BUILDING BRAND VALUE THE PLAYBOY WAY

Titles by the same author

Google Blogger for Dummies
Harry Potter: The Story of a Global Business Phenomenon
Kick-ass Copywriting in 10 Easy Steps

BUILDING BRAND VALUE THE PLAYBOY WAY

Susan Gunelius

*President & CEO,
KeySplash Creative, Inc.*

palgrave
macmillan

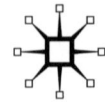

© Susan Gunelius 2009
© Foreword by Allen P. Adamson

All rights reserved. No reproduction, copy or transmission of this publication may be made without written permission.

No portion of this publication may be reproduced, copied or transmitted save with written permission or in accordance with the provisions of the Copyright, Designs and Patents Act 1988, or under the terms of any licence permitting limited copying issued by the Copyright Licensing Agency, Saffron House, 6-10 Kirby Street, London EC1N 8TS.

Any person who does any unauthorized act in relation to this publication may be liable to criminal prosecution and civil claims for damages.

The author has asserted her right to be identified as the author of this work in accordance with the Copyright, Designs and Patents Act 1988.

First published 2009 by
PALGRAVE MACMILLAN

Palgrave Macmillan in the UK is an imprint of Macmillan Publishers Limited, registered in England, company number 785998, of Houndmills, Basingstoke, Hampshire RG21 6XS.

Palgrave Macmillan in the US is a division of St Martin's Press LLC, 175 Fifth Avenue, New York, NY 10010.

Palgrave Macmillan is the global academic imprint of the above companies and has companies and representatives throughout the world.

Palgrave® and Macmillan® are registered trademarks in the United States, the United Kingdom, Europe and other countries.

ISBN-13: 978–0–230–57789–3

This book is printed on paper suitable for recycling and made from fully managed and sustained forest sources. Logging, pulping and manufacturing processes are expected to conform to the environmental regulations of the country of origin.

A catalogue record for this book is available from the British Library.

A catalog record for this book is available from the Library of Congress.

10 9 8 7 6 5 4 3 2 1
18 17 16 15 14 13 12 11 10 09

Printed and bound in China

To Scott for watching The Girls Next Door *with me and encouraging me to turn my thoughts into this book.*

CONTENTS

List of illustrations		x
Foreword		xii
Preface		xv
Acknowledgements		xvii
Introduction	Warning: This Book is Not about Sex	xviii

Part I Reinventing an Industry—The Years up to 1959

Chapter 1	**The Brand Dream**		**3**
	Modest Beginnings		3
	The First Reinvention of Hugh Hefner		5
	Hugh Hefner's Self-Exploration		6
	The Turning Point		8
	Bringing the Dream to Life		10
Chapter 2	**A Brand is Born**		**12**
	One Part Risk, One Part Belief, and One Part Good Luck		13
	Early Promotion Tactics		15
Chapter 3	**Nurturing a Brand**		**20**
	Understanding the Environment in the 1950s		21
	Keeping up with Brand Growth		22
	Hugh Hefner Reinvents Himself Again and the Ultimate Brand Champion Arrives		24

CONTENTS

| Chapter 4 | **The First Brand Extensions** | 26 |
| | Playboy Defies Marketing Rules | 28 |

Part II A Brand Rises Despite the Naysayers—The 1960s

Chapter 5	**Growth Explosion**	37
	A Brand Grows Too Big	40
Chapter 6	**Defending the Brand**	47
	The Playboy Philosophy	49
	Playboy as an Inclusive Brand	50
Chapter 7	**Living the Brand**	55
	Hugh Hefner Reinvents Himself for the Third Time	58
	Playboy as a Cult Brand	60

Part III A Brand Goes Global—The 1970s

Chapter 8	**The Brand Seen and Protested Around the World**	67
	A Brand on the Defensive	69
	Playboy Goes Global	71
Chapter 9	**A Brand Peaks**	74
	Competitive Attacks against the Pioneer Brand	75
	Signs of Brand Trouble Become a Reality	82
Chapter 10	**A Brand Sees the Error of Its Ways and Tries to Give Back**	87
	Changing Course and Saving Face Through Brand Building	90
	Facing a Segment Market	91

Part IV A Brand in Decline—The 1980s

Chapter 11	**A Changing World**	95
	Politics vs. Playboy in the 1980s	95
	Society vs. Playboy in the 1980s	97
	The Longevity of the Playboy Brand	98
Chapter 12	**A Changing of the Guard**	103
	The Meese Report Attacks Playboy	105
	Christie Hefner Takes Control	106
Chapter 13	**A Change of Course**	112
	Controversy Takes a Toll on the Brand Champion	112
	A Turn to Merchandising	115

CONTENTS

Moving into Television	118
The Brand Champion Shocks the World	120

Part V Reinventing a Brand—The 1990s

Chapter 14 A New Focus — 123
- Hugh Hefner Retains Control of *Playboy* Magazine — 124
- Celebrities and Playboy — 128
- *Playboy* Magazine by the Numbers in the 1990s — 130

Chapter 15 New Brand Extensions — 133
- Global Expansion of Playboy — 134
- Expanding the Television and Video Segments of Playboy Enterprises — 135
- Expanding Playboy Merchandise — 138
- Playboy Online — 139

Chapter 16 The Brand Champion Returns to the Spotlight — 141
- Competition Grows — 143
- Leveraging an Integrated Marketing Strategy — 144

Part VI A Brand Rises Back to the Top—The 2000s and the Future

Chapter 17 A Brand for a New Generation — 151
- Competition, the Macro Environment and the Girls Next Door — 154

Chapter 18 A Relationship Brand History in Review — 159
- Developing a Brand — 163
- Extending a Brand — 165
- A Brand Comes Full Circle — 166

Chapter 19 The Future of the Playboy Brand — 168
- Hugh Hefner—The Ultimate Brand Champion — 172
- What's Next for Playboy — 173

Bibliography — 177

Index — 183

ILLUSTRATIONS

TABLES

I	Timeline—The 1950s	1
II	Timeline—The 1960s	35
III	Timeline—The 1970s	65
IV	Timeline—The 1980s	93
V	Timeline—The 1990s	121
VI	Timeline—The 2000s	149

FIGURES

4.1	Four orders of brand experience	33
7.1	The three stages of consumer emotional involvement	62

BOXES

1.1	The creation of the Playboy bunny logo	11
2.1	The Silent Generation	14
2.2	Understanding relationship branding	18
4.1	Defining an experience brand	30
4.2	Consumer emotional involvement theory	32
5.1	The Hard Rock Cafe and Jack Daniels as experience brands	40
5.2	Brand extension strategies and risks	41

5.3	Examples of brands forced to contract	44
6.1	The Baby Boomer Generation	48
6.2	"I Was a Playboy Bunny" by Gloria Steinem	52
6.3	How Toyota and Pepsi leveraged the macro environment with different results	53
7.1	Celebrities and writers in Playboy during the 1960s	56
7.2	The inclusive brand strategy of Barack Obama's 2008 U.S. Presidential Campaign	60
7.3	Cult brands	61
8.1	Generation Jones	68
9.1	Competitive market positioning strategies	76
9.2	Offensive and defensive positioning strategies	78
9.3	Brands that failed to meet customer expectations	81
9.4	Brand expansion without restraint	83
10.1	Awards and honors bestowed upon Hugh Hefner during the 1970s	89
11.1	Brands that faced decline and survived with mixed results	99
11.2	Brand survival stories	101
12.1	The repositioning of Clorox and Hyundai	110
13.1	Awards and honors bestowed upon Hugh Hefner during the 1980s	114
13.2	Success stories of extending and merchandising brands	116
13.3	The Hallmark Channel	119
14.1	Generation X	127
14.2	The power of celebrity brand endorsements	129
15.1	United States vs. Playboy Entertainment Group, Inc.	137
16.1	Awards and honors bestowed on Hugh Hefner in the 1990s	142
16.2	Integrated marketing in business	144
17.1	Generation Y	153
17.2	*Interns*	158
18.1	Steve Jobs: The Apple brand champion	161
18.2	Mary Kay Ash: The Mary Kay brand champion	162
18.3	Awards and honors bestowed on Hugh Hefner in the 2000s	163
19.1	Skoal and Playboy	174

FOREWORD

Ask any man who has read *Playboy* magazine at some point in his life and he'll most likely tell you with a wink and a nod that "it's for the fiction." While the esteemed writers who contributed stories and essays to the publication include no less than the likes of Kurt Vonnegut, Norman Mailer, Saul Bellow, and John Steinbeck, the notion that anyone has *ever* read *Playboy* solely for the fiction is, well, a fiction. From its inception, men have enjoyed *Playboy* magazine because it represented one of the most well-defined and differentiated brand promises of the 20th century. It was an experience built upon a simple, yet meticulously planned and implemented brand idea: every man's dream of the good life. In its heyday, Playboy, the magazine and the empire, was a brand like no other. In fact, it may well have been in a brand class by itself.

That Playboy has achieved renown as a global brand is no accident. Its success is the result of founder Hugh Hefner's adherence to the rules of Branding 101. With no formal background in brand management, Hefner still understood that strong brands are not built on logos, clever and ubiquitous as his turned out to be, but on a set of mental associations brought to life through a spectrum of carefully aligned experiences. From my own, more formal background in brand management, I can tell you that Susan Gunelius', engaging new book, *The Playboy Brand*, is not just a great tale skillfully told, but also a perfect lesson for anyone interested in what it takes to build a powerful brand, regardless of the category.

While he started the multimillion-dollar Playboy enterprise with $600 and a desire to challenge the repressive sexual attitudes of his day, Hefner's ultimate achievement was his ability to identify a unique idea, a promise that was both different from any other in the category (no smut, please), and relevant to the target market. In addition, it was his ability to envision and put into play the array of experiences necessary to genuinely bring this idea to life. He understood that everything associated with the promise had to hold together from touch point to touch point, from one branding element to the next in order to be perceived as credible.

That this happened is legend. Hef's simple brand idea, actually articulated in a serialized manifesto entitled the *Playboy Philosophy*, was about as fine a strategic branding document as can be found in any top-notch marketing firm. Every man's dream of the urban, urbane lifestyle, the activities, manners and morés it embodied, were soundly articulated. Hefner's belief that life should be a celebration, a cool embrace of sexy merry-making and marvelously uninhibited beautiful women (though innocent enough to take home to mom), of superior wining and dining, good grooming, good music and good times, was as watertight a rendition of brand guidelines as exists – and men lived it and loved it. From branding applications that included clubs and restaurants, mansions, resorts and jets, and, yes, those endearing Bunnies (whom you actually *can't* touch), Hefner orchestrated and continues to vet the totality of the Playboy brand experience with an eye for detail and the conducting skill of a maestro.

Leaving nothing to chance, Hefner maintains his role as chief brand champion to this day; another basic rule followed by successful brand owners. Be it founder, CEO, CMO, or HR director, all winning brands have someone who is a chief brand advocate, cheerleader, and seer. Someone who ensures that every person associated with the brand knows what it stands for and what it means to keep its promise. Hef's voice is the voice of the brand, whether it comes straight from the man in the silk robe and ascot, or is implied in the décor of the Playboy Mansion and Clubs, the demeanor of the lucky folks who work for the company, at the restaurants or exotic travel locales recommended by its publications, or the counsel of that sage *Playboy Advisor*. Playboy and its founder are as inextricably woven as are all the experiences of the brand itself.

Playboy is an iconic global brand and Gunelius' book explains how it achieved this status. With the tenets of branding as backdrop, she demonstrates how, in the age of the pill and the dawning of sexual freedom, Hefner saw a unique opportunity to challenge the old

FOREWORD

"stag rags" with a brand that was not about unclad girls but, rather, an acceptable and accessible urban male fantasy (just this side of naughty) which he brought to life with class and wit. He saw a gap in the marketplace and, with a simple, well-defined brand idea as foundation, created a variety of perfectly interwoven experiences to fill it. He was, and is, the brand's champion and prophet, a voice not just of the brand, but for the brand. In Gunelius' hands, the story of Playboy, the brand and man behind it, are worth reading for both fun and the lessons learned.

ALLEN P. ADAMSON
Managing Director
Landor Associates
Author: *Brand Simple* and *Brand Digital*

PREFACE

This book is about the history of a brand—Playboy. Therefore, it is written chronologically by decade with each Part representing a different decade in the Playboy brand lifecycle. However, this book is not a biography, nor is it an annotated timeline of events. Instead, it is written with a focus on branding theory and the marketing strategies and tactics that create, develop, expand, revive, and sustain a brand.

Each chapter within a Part concentrates on specific aspects of branding or the brand lifecycle within that corresponding decade. That means you are likely to find marketing tactics and strategies referred to in multiple chapters as they apply to different periods in the Playboy brand lifecycle. For example, Playboy's online endeavors in the 2000s are discussed in Chapter 17 as they relate to repositioning the Playboy brand for a new generation of consumers as well as in Chapter 18 as they relate to relationship branding. Similarly, relationship branding is discussed in many chapters as Playboy's position as a relationship brand evolved over the course of the brand's lifecycle.

The chapters within this book were written with discussion and analysis in mind. As you read each chapter, be prepared to question the tactics the company used to grow and sustain the brand. Consider how the brand was affected by the macro environment it was expected to perform in and the decisions made by the Playboy company to overcome obstacles and take the brand into the next decade. Also, examine the role that Hugh Hefner played throughout the Playboy brand lifecycle. It's an incredible branding story. Furthermore, each part includes a variety of examples from other well-known brands and companies to help put some marketing and branding theories into better perspective

PREFACE

and provides a basis for comparison where it can be useful. These are just a few of the topics that will be addressed throughout this book that marketers and business people can learn from and apply to their own worlds.

Before you dive into the story of the Playboy brand, I need to mention that all product, company, and brand names are trademarks of their respective owners. Also, I apologize for any instances where copyrighted material has been used inadvertently where permission was not obtained and am happy to rectify the omission in future editions. Finally, this book is not authorized by Hugh Hefner, Playboy Enterprises, or any of its affiliates or employees. Instead, this book is about my personal analysis and opinions based on marketing theory of how one man's $8,000 investment turned into one of the most well-recognized and talked about brands in history and created the ultimate brand champion.

There is a reason that Playboy has survived for so long, and there is a reason the Playboy brand remains strong despite its fluctuating stock performance. There are lessons to learn from Playboy and Hugh Hefner. It's a fascinating story that anyone interested in business, branding, marketing, or Playboy can learn from, so without further ado, let's get started!

SUSAN GUNELIUS
February 2009

ACKNOWLEDGMENTS

It's always challenging to narrow down the list of people who helped get a book into readers' hands into a page or two of acknowledgments, and this book is not an exception. First, I have to acknowledge my agent, Bob Diforio, and Stephen Rutt at Palgrave Macmillan for letting me write this book. I'm thrilled that both Bob and Stephen recognized that despite the controversy that often comes with Playboy, the marketing and branding story is one that both students and professionals can learn from for many years to come.

On a personal note, I have to acknowledge my husband, Scott, who works so hard to take care of our children, our house, and our lives while I write (and that's on top of his full-time job). Without his help, I would not be able to write books or run my company, KeySplash Creative, Inc. To Scott, I love you!

For when they are old enough to read this, I have to acknowledge my children, Brynn, Daniel, and Ryan who make the hard work worth it with their smiling faces. I love you.

Finally, thank you to my parents, Bill and Carol Ann Henry, for supporting me and being such an important part of my family's lives. We're so lucky to have you, and I love you.

INTRODUCTION

WARNING: THIS BOOK IS NOT ABOUT SEX

What's the first thing you think of when you hear the word, *Playboy*? If you said *sex*, then you're just one of hundreds of millions of people around the world who make the same association, and I'm going to tell you two things right now based on that association:

1. The Playboy brand is working.
2. This book is not about sex.

Of course, if you didn't answer the above question with the word *sex*, then I'm very curious to know what your answer was. Regardless, I didn't write this book to talk about sex. This book is about branding and marketing. It's about the history of an iconic, globally powerful brand that represents an unlikely subject for a product that has gone from highly controversial to somewhat of a commodity over the course of half a century. Most importantly, this book is about the role of a brand champion in building a brand.

For Playboy, Hugh Hefner played the role of brand champion throughout the brand's 55+ year lifecycle. It could be argued that there has been no other brand champion in history who could be so closely associated with the brand he championed, nor is there another brand champion who has fulfilled that role for such a long period of time. Other brand champion names such as Steve Jobs, Mary Kay Ash, Oprah Winfrey, Bill Gates, and Martha Stewart come to mind, and many of those people will be discussed in this book. However, they all pale in

INTRODUCTION

comparison to Hugh Hefner who became the living embodiment of the Playboy brand.

I should mention that Hefner's role as brand champion was one he played with vigor and resolute purpose. But as some might wonder how his stamina endures in his private life, I wonder how his stamina to champion the Playboy brand in the public's eye and through his workaholic behavior continues to drive him. As you read this book, you'll learn more about Hugh Hefner, the man. You'll learn how his childhood shaped his thinking and much of his behavior, and you'll learn what that meant to the Playboy brand. You'll learn how his belief in the product he created, Playboy, was all-encompassing, and you'll learn how he promoted and defended the brand and company above all else as a tireless brand advocate and brand guardian.

However, this book is not a biography of Hugh Hefner's life. On the contrary, this book is an analysis of the lifecycle of a powerful brand led by the ultimate brand champion. Marketers and branding experts are always searching for the perfect recipe to boost brand equity. There is no doubt that a powerful brand can be an invaluable company asset, however, marketers have always battled with senior management to secure the budget necessary to build brand value. The reason is simple. Brands are intangible assets. Company owners, shareholders, and analysts want to see hard numbers reflected on balance sheets and income statements. Unfortunately, there is no space in accounting software for "Brand" to fit in the Assets column. That doesn't make it any less meaningful and useful, but companies focus on metrics and quantifiable data. Things like brand fall to the wayside. It's an unfortunate reality in the profit-driven, bottom-line conscious world of business. Building brand equity is a long-term strategy. When shareholders demand double-digit growth year over year, corporate executives typically choose short-term tactics to meet those expectations and keep their jobs over long-term strategies to position the company for continued success in the future.

This book is meant to demonstrate how the power of a brand can sustain a company through the ups and downs of a company's history. All days weren't perfect in the history of Playboy. In fact, much of the past 30 years have been bleak for Playboy, however, the company survived. Despite facing a wide variety of challenges, not the least of which has been an inability to be proactive and develop long-term strategies, Playboy has survived. How? This book will show you that a strong brand can help a company weather the storms and overcome insurmountable obstacles.

INTRODUCTION

Don't get me wrong. A strong brand doesn't guarantee success, but the power of a well-established, well-known brand can boost a company's chances for success immensely. Did anyone think that Martha Stewart's company could fully rebound after she was found guilty of violating insider trading laws and spent several months in prison? Many people thought her business would fail after its brand champion brought such public humiliation to the company. However, the public was able to disassociate Stewart's personal financial troubles from her brand's promise. The company rebounded and her stint in jail is remembered as a mere diversion in the brand's lifecycle.

Similarly, did anyone believe that Tylenol could regain its stronghold in the over-the-counter pain reliever market after the Tylenol poisoning epidemic in the 1980s? The brand seemed tarnished beyond repair, yet within a very short time, the company not only repaired the product's brand image but it reclaimed its place as market leader. Again, the power of a brand cannot be denied.

The Playboy brand overcame a myriad of obstacles during its lifecycle. Despite being linked to violent sex crimes, a murder, drugs, and more, the brand emerged from each attack strong and continued to grow. Much of that success can be attributed to Hugh Hefner as the ultimate brand champion continually defending the brand. His utter belief in his product and brand was tenacious. In fact, many people found it hard not to believe in him.

That leads to one of the most important aspects of the longevity of the Playboy brand. At its core, Playboy is a relationship brand, and relationship brands are always well-positioned to become extremely powerful. As you'll learn in this book, a relationship brand invites people to personally connect with it, directly interact with it, and share brand experiences with others. Relationship brands typically lead to strong customer loyalty, and loyal consumers turn into repeat buyers and brand advocates. There is no more powerful form of word-of-mouth marketing than a band of loyal brand advocate customers. They talk about the brand they're loyal to with others, defend it, and buy it again and again. There is a reason why that old Breck shampoo commercial used the tagline, "and she told two friends, and so on, and so on, and so on." It just works.

Even if you detest pornography and would never purchase a product sold by Playboy, it's undeniable that the brand is powerful and has lived a long and prosperous life. And there is no denying that much of the brand's success can be linked directly to Hugh Hefner. So did I pique your curiosity? Want to learn more? Keep reading!

PART I

REINVENTING AN INDUSTRY—THE YEARS UP TO 1959

TABLE I **Timeline—The 1950s**

1953: With $8,000, Hugh Hefner launches *Playboy* with the first issue featuring nude photos of Marilyn Monroe as the "Sweetheart of the Month." 56,000 copies are sold of 70,000 printed.

1954: The second issue of *Playboy* hits newsstands in January and the "Sweetheart of the Month" is renamed the "Playmate of the Month."

1955: *Playboy* is the 80th largest selling magazine in the United States. First major advertiser, Springmaid, signs on.

1956: *Playboy* grows by 102% to become the 49th largest selling magazine in the United States. Centerfold enters popular lexicon.

1957: Hugh Hefner legally separates from his first wife and becomes the subject of a June article in *Playboy* magazine depicting him as the real-life Playboy. FBI begins investigating Hugh Hefner based on his liberal views about sex.

1958: Research study by Daniel Starch & Staff reports *Playboy* readers spend more money than readers of any other magazine.

1959: Hugh Hefner's divorce is finalized. *Playboy* circulation rises above 1 million copies per month. Chicago Playboy Mansion is purchased; *Playboy's Penthouse* television program debuts. Playboy Jazz Festival premieres.

CHAPTER 1

THE BRAND DREAM

We would not be sitting here today if I called it "Stag Party."
Hugh Hefner, May 19, 1983 Interview
with Greg Jackson on ABC News

Say what you will about Hugh Hefner, the man had a vision, took the steps to make the vision become a reality, and succeeded despite the challenges he faced. It can't hurt that he has an IQ of 152—genius level, which was determined through an IQ test he took as a child. Truth be told, intelligence can be a benefit or a liability when it comes to being an entrepreneur. While it can help a person make sound decisions, it can also prohibit him from taking risks. It goes along with the old adage, "too much information can be dangerous," but in the case of entrepreneurs, too much information can be limiting because it can create artificial barriers. The best entrepreneurs can balance the facts, risks, and potential rewards to make sound business decisions. Hugh Hefner brought the tools of intelligence to the table, but when married with his belief in his product and his ability to accept risks, his men's lifestyle magazine grew to become one of the most iconic brands in modern history.

MODEST BEGINNINGS

It might surprise some people to learn that Hugh Marston Hefner, born in Chicago, Illinois on April 9, 1926, is related to well-known Massachusetts Puritan leaders—William Bradford and John Winthrop.

REINVENTING AN INDUSTRY—THE YEARS UP TO 1959

Both men are historical figures who played major roles in the early days of settling the Plymouth colony in the United States in the 1600s. It's an ironic ancestral link that may have played a bigger role in the shaping of Hugh Hefner's life and the Playboy brand than one might realize.

Hugh Hefner grew up in a household that was dominated by conservative Protestant thinking. Hefner's parents, Glenn and Grace Hefner, raised Hefner and his younger brother, Keith, just like most other parents did in the first half of the 1900s. It was a time when human sexuality was highly repressed. Even discussions of the human body were off-limits. The hypocrisy of the time did not go unnoticed to the young Hugh Hefner, but he led the majority of his childhood years unnerved by the sexless doctrine of the world (at least in the public's eye) where sex was viewed merely as a means to an end.

Hefner's father played a big role in the development of his elder son's personality. Glenn Hefner held a job in the corporate world of Chicago where he made a decent salary that allowed his family to live comfortably. However, Glenn was a workaholic who rarely saw his children and spent the vast majority of his time at his office. The fact that Hugh Hefner, himself, would grow up to be addicted to his work is not surprising.

On the contrary, Grace Hefner was always available to Hugh and Keith Hefner, albeit a conservative and repressed availability. Grace Hefner was college educated but played the role of stay-at-home mother rather than pursuing her own career. Her duties were to raise the children and keep the house in order, and she performed both well. Grace was an interesting woman who not only followed a strict, nearly Puritanical doctrine of behavior but also embraced science and social thinking. In theory, Grace represented an inner struggle that many men and women experienced during the first half of the 20th century when they began questioning repressive social morés and craving more personal freedom.

Hefner was always a shy child, a trait that would follow him through adulthood. His mother parented by giving him everything he wanted, and Hefner grew up with an expectation that he should always get his way. His self-obsessed personality would become the cornerstone of his personal brand in later years. During his childhood and into his adult life, Hefner found comfort in movies, music and pop culture, and fantasized about the lives of the people he watched on-screen. It was during his childhood years that Hefner began displaying a creative side, drawing cartoons, and writing poems and stories, all of which would become an important part of his path to launching *Playboy* magazine. He spent much of his childhood living inside his own head, a characteristic that got him into trouble at school numerous times and fed his self-absorption.

As a result of Hefner's shy nature, he preferred to stir the proverbial pot and then sit back and watch people react and participate in activities as he continued to stoke the fire. It could be argued that this voyeuristic nature is at the heart of the Playboy product, and that's probably quite accurate. After all, the Playboy brand mission is meant to create a fantasy and help readers learn how to live those fantasies in their own lives. In his youth, Hefner expressed his voyeuristic nature through his cartoons and ventured into his first entrepreneurial effort at the tender age of 8 or 9 when he typed his own newspaper and sold it door-to-door for one cent per copy.

THE FIRST REINVENTION OF HUGH HEFNER

It wasn't until Hefner reached his teenage years that he decided to take a step in a new direction and reinvented himself. It's a process he'd repeat numerous times in his life where he shed one skin for another, thereby repositioning his personal brand just as he would the Playboy brand over the years. Repositioning a brand is essential to maintaining its relevancy with the inevitably changing marketplace. Hefner's ability to reinvent and reposition himself would prove invaluable throughout his life and career and would help to keep the Playboy brand alive for over half a century and counting.

Hugh Hefner's first self-reinvention happened during his junior year of high school. When the girl he liked refused his request for a date, he decided to make some drastic changes in his life. He adopted a new nickname, Hef, changed his wardrobe, changed the way he spoke, and became his fantasy of what a popular teenager should be. His efforts worked, and soon he and his closest friend became the leaders of the "in" crowd. In his senior year, he was elected president of his school's student council and received numerous accolades in the classic "Most Likely To..." awards that don many yearbooks to this day. Among Hefner's top three showings bestowed upon him by his classmates were, "Most Likely to Succeed," "Most Popular Boy," "Class Humorist," "Best Orator," "Best Dancer," and "Most Artistic," (Watts, p. 30). Hefner's popularity soared, and so did his ego. Suddenly, he realized that there was more to life, and it was within his reach.

Hefner's newfound self-confidence and popularity parlayed themselves into a chronicle of his own life, which he would obsessively work on throughout his entire life in one form or another. In an ultimate act of self-absorption, Hefner created a cartoon character of himself named Goo Heffer. He combined his love of drawing cartoons, writing stories, and himself into what's been called a cartoon autobiography. In essence, he was creating his personal brand, at least the vision of his personal brand that he wanted to attain, through his stories of Goo Heffer. The cartoon focused on Goo Heffer's school days, friends, and girls. Throughout the story, Goo Heffer was always the central figure around whom the world revolved. Other characters loved him and wanted to be in the presence of this ultimate suave, cool guy. It seems that even at this early age, Hugh Hefner clearly knew where he wanted his life to go. He just didn't know how to get there yet.

At the same time, Hugh Hefner began speaking out against ideas and activities he thought were oppressive and robbed people of the freedoms he believed they ought to have. He spoke out against restrictions related to music and dancing that were commonplace in high schools during the 1940s. He vocally questioned societal rules that viewed premarital sex or overt sexual behavior as immoral.

In his early teens, Hefner discovered *Esquire* magazine, a men's lifestyle magazine that included sexual cartoons and images which piqued the young boy's interest in women. Like boys from all generations, he hung those pictures on his bedroom walls and idolized them. He wanted to live the life depicted in the pages of *Esquire* magazine. In fact, he wanted to lead a life one step *beyond* the life described in *Esquire*. It was his love of drawing and his desire for a different kind of life, combined with his strong feelings for personal freedom, particularly sexual freedom, that would drive him throughout his adult years.

HUGH HEFNER'S SELF-EXPLORATION

Hugh Hefner's childhood played out while society navigated the aftermaths of prohibition and the Great Depression, and his years as a teenager and young adult would continue to be greatly affected by world events. Hugh Hefner graduated from high school in 1944 in the midst of World War II, and like all other young American men, he was expected to serve his country in the war overseas. He left high school behind and got prepared to enter the U.S. Army.

THE BRAND DREAM

As luck would have it, he met the woman who would eventually become his first wife, Mildred Williams, just two weeks before he had to report for duty. As with all aspects of Hefner's young life, his romance with Millie Williams became a fantasy he obsessively had to fulfill. He left to report for his army duty not only with a desire to carry out his obligation but also with an utter distaste of change of any kind, particularly change that he did not initiate. Again, this is a characteristic that would follow him throughout his life. However, he wasn't prepared for the eye-opening experience his stint in the army would deliver.

Entering the army brought the naive Hefner in touch with people from all walks of life. Suddenly, he witnessed prejudices he had never been exposed to before. His fairly sheltered upbringing didn't prepare him for the open prejudice he would see from many of the new people around him. He realized at this time that he was actually very fortunate and discovered another area where fundamental freedoms were not being met—equality. It's a subject that would come up repeatedly throughout his career as the embodiment of the Playboy brand. Frequent attacks against Hefner and the Playboy brand as being oppressive to women would be countered voraciously by Hefner who felt his magazine depicted quite the opposite.

Surprisingly, the army would also be the place where Hugh Hefner's creative vision was allowed to blossom. Just as he prepared to ship out for active overseas duty as an infantry rifleman, he received word that his assignment had changed. Instead of crossing the ocean with a rifle in hand, he would sit at a desk with a typewriter at his fingertips. Hefner was assigned to a desk job, thanks to his speedy typing skills. Had his typing prowess not been noticed, Hugh Hefner's life may have been radically different. However, his new desk job provided him two important opportunities that would help shape his future—he spent much time with the young women of Washington, D.C. (despite his obsession with Millie Williams), and he spent much time working on his cartoons and creative endeavors.

Luckily for Hugh Hefner, he would never have to set foot on foreign soil during World War II. The war ended, and in 1946, a 20-year-old Hugh Hefner returned to Chicago where he, like many veterans returning from service, struggled to find himself again.

Not one to do anything without giving 200% (refer to the previously discussed obsessive personality), Hugh Hefner decided to enroll in college at the University of Chicago at Urbana where Millie Williams was a student. However, a regular 4-year stint wasn't good enough for Hugh

Hefner. Instead, he found a way to get his degree in just 2 1/2 years. He studied psychology, not because he wanted to work in the field of psychology (he wanted to be a cartoonist), but because he was obsessed with human behavior stemming from his repressive upbringing, experiences of prejudice witnessed during his time with the army, and his desire for basic freedom of behavior (particularly self-gratification—a theme that carried through Hugh Hefner's entire life).

A psychology major didn't stop Hefner from continuing his love of cartooning and art. His plan remained the same, and his dream was to be a cartoonist. He kept plenty of time open between his studies to pursue those personal interests. Hefner became very involved in two campus publications, the *Daily Illini* (the student paper) and *Shaft* (a humorous campus magazine) where he contributed cartoons and later acted in editorial roles. In addition, he continued to chronicle his life through Goo Heffer and a growing scrapbook collection dedicated to every event in his life, including college football stories, cartoons, and more.

THE TURNING POINT

It's often said that there are many defining moments in history. The same can be said of Hugh Hefner's life and the fate of what would ultimately become his legacy, Playboy. In 1948, *Sexual Behavior in the Human Male* was published by Alfred Kinsey. The book caused a buzz that was fueled by controversy. Never before had the topics of sex and sexuality been discussed in such an open and honest way; it could be called the most politically incorrect book of its time and broke down barriers in terms of taking a taboo subject and making people talk about it, either positively or negatively. Hugh Hefner was deeply affected by *Sexual Behavior in the Human Male*, which put down on paper and justified many of the thoughts and feelings he had and knew other people had as well. As usual, Hugh Hefner became obsessed with Kinsey's book, and it became a guiding influence in his life.

Reading *Sexual Behavior in the Human Male* was an epiphany for a 22-year-old Hugh Hefner, and its frank discussion of sex led Hefner to push the envelope with his own creative work. In fact, his first step toward Playboy came while he was still in college and introduced a Coed of the Month feature to *Shaft*, his college humor magazine. He began speaking about sex to anyone who would listen and advocated bringing more sexual material to *Shaft*. His final year in college was marked by his all-consuming interest in sex and Kinsey's report.

Hefner graduated from college in February 1949 with no job and a relationship on rocky grounds. Marrying Millie Williams 4 months later wouldn't help Hefner find his path anytime soon. Like many young people who leave the secure walls of a college campus to brave the real world, Hugh Hefner didn't know what to do with himself. He loved to draw but had no idea how to get a job using his passion and talent. He took a job he hated as an employment manager for the Chicago Carton Company simply to make money. Within 5 months he quit, in part due to the company's mistreatment of minorities.

Hefner tried to seek security by entering graduate school, but left after one semester. Next, he took a job as a copywriter for the Carson, Pirie, Scott department store, but left after 6 months. Finally, a job as a copywriter for his beloved *Esquire* seemed like a step in the right direction, but the confines of a 9-to-5 job were too rigid. He quit when employees were moved to New York City and Hefner's request for a $5 raise was denied. Once again, he found himself on the periphery of his fantasy life that he dreamed of with no hope of getting inside.

Hefner's next foray into the publishing world was an important one that played a significant role in his later career. In 1952, he took a job with Publisher's Department Corporation as the manager of promotions and circulation. Suddenly, he found himself learning a new side of the magazine publishing industry and gaining valuable knowledge that would help him later when he would start his own magazine. However, Hefner again felt stifled and quit. In 1953, he found employment as a promotions manager for *Children's Activities* magazine where he was still unhappy but was earning a bit more money to support his family.

Throughout the course of his aimless job-hopping during his early career, Hefner continued to pursue his creative interests. He tried to sell two comic strips without success, and he picked up a gig writing movie reviews for a local magazine. His single success during this time came when he published a book of his own satirical cartoons in 1951 called *That Toddlin' Town: A Rowdy Burlesque of Chicago Manners and Morals*. The book was a local success, and Hefner was bitten by the media-attention bug. It also gave him the confidence to believe he could start his own magazine. But his plans would be delayed when Millie discovered she was pregnant.

Christie Hefner was born in November 1952 and David Hefner arrived 3 years later. During that time, Hugh Hefner spent long hours working, similar to his own father's behavior during his childhood, and spent less and less time with his family. However, on a pivotal winter night in early 1953, a 26-year-old Hugh Hefner made the decision to change his life. He would put his dream to start his own magazine into action and let the chips fall where they may.

BRINGING THE DREAM TO LIFE

Using his experiences at *Esquire*, the Publisher's Development Corporation, and his other jobs that he had deemed fairly useless up to this point in his life, Hugh Hefner created a concept for a magazine that would deliver the kinds of information and images *he* would be interested in, and he was confident there were many more people just like him who would be equally interested. At the core of the magazine would be the topic of sex; the hook—semi-nude photos of beautiful women, the payoff—a tasteful magazine that provided useful and interesting content for men who wanted to live a sophisticated lifestyle.

Hefner had everything figured out from the content to the style, the layout to the competition, the audience to the delivery, and everything in between. He invested a significant amount of effort into creating the actual product and formed his own publishing company, HMH Publishing Company. Using his limited knowledge of the publishing industry from his earlier forays into the business, he secured advance orders and distribution points as well as great content.

His passion for his subject and his product were inescapable, and with little effort he was able to convince friends and former coworkers to help him achieve his dream. He secured a $600 loan using his furniture as collateral and obtained additional loans from family members and friends (including his mother who didn't believe in the product but did believe in her son). Ultimately, he had $8,000 and a dream. It was a big risk, and he knew it. However, he believed so strongly in his product that he risked his family's livelihood for it. With some sense of security in Millie's job as a teacher, Hefner worked day and night to make his dream a reality.

As Hefner worked on his new magazine, he hoped he held potential gold in his hands. He was confident with his hook and his concept but knew he needed bait to draw attention to the first issue. Originally, he planned to use a nude photo of a woman in 3D, which was very popular in the early 1950s, as bait, but another pivotal moment occurred when Hefner discovered he had an opportunity to purchase the rights to previously unpublished nude photographs of Marilyn Monroe whose career was skyrocketing. Knowing a huge opportunity when

> **BOX 1.1 The creation of the Playboy bunny logo**
>
> When Hugh Hefner was faced with a last minute dilemma that forced him to change the name and icon for his new magazine, he settled on *Playboy* at a friend's suggestion. The rabbit was chosen to be the *Playboy* icon because Hefner believed it represented a playfulness that suited the magazine. An artist drew the iconic logo that is famous around the globe to this day in half an hour. At Hefner's request, a bow-tie was added to the bunny image in order to give the logo a classier feel.
>
> The simple, timeless logo grew to represent the Playboy brand message, image, and promise for multiple generations, cultures, and societies, demonstrating that a logo is just one component of a brand but when used effectively and consistently, it can become an invaluable asset.

he saw it, Hugh Hefner left nothing to chance. He got in his car and drove to the John Baumgarth Calendar Company of Chicago where he made a deal to purchase the photos for just $600. With nude photos of Marilyn Monroe in hand, Hefner finished putting together the first issue of *Playboy* on his kitchen table.

Hefner's first issue of his new magazine would feature Marilyn Monroe on the cover and in a pictorial inside the magazine. The original name for the magazine was *Stag Party*, but a last minute cease and desist demand from *Stag Magazine*, an outdoor adventure magazine, forced Hefner to change the name and the symbolic icon of the magazine. *Stag Party* changed to *Playboy* and the stag icon changed to a bunny with a tuxedo tie—a brand name and brand icon that would eventually become recognized around the world as one of the most powerful relationship brands in history (see Box 1.1 for more information about the creation of the Playboy logo).

Again, relying on contacts he had made during his previous jobs in the publishing field, Hefner was able to negotiate a printing arrangement partially on credit, and 70,000 copies of the first issue of *Playboy* rolled off the presses in time for a December 1953 launch. The dice had been rolled and the risks had been taken. No one knew at that time that the magazine they held in their hands would become a worldwide success.

CHAPTER 2

A BRAND IS BORN

It was much less a calculated business move than it was how I wanted to live.

Hugh Hefner, 1983 Interview
with Charlie Rose

The first week of December 1953 marked a time that would change Hugh Hefner's life and the lives of people around the world in the coming decades. As 70,000 copies of *Playboy's* inaugural issue made their way to newsstands, a 27-year-old Hefner crossed his fingers and hoped the rest of the world was ready for it. The new magazine Hefner delivered took his much-adored *Esquire* to the next level—a level he thought young men were prepared to enter with him. The repressive social morés he grew up with were representative of what he referred to as a "hurtful hypocrisy" from which he hoped to free the world. Would the world be ready for it?

Hefner's question was answered quickly as 56,000 copies of the first issue of *Playboy* sold out in a very short time. With initial success fueling Hefner, he released the second issue of *Playboy*, and it outsold the first issue by 2,000 copies. *Playboy* filled a niche and affirmed Hefner's belief that society was ready for a significant change in terms of its views toward sexuality.

However, Hefner never believed *Playboy* was a magazine about sex. On the contrary, Hefner believed from the beginning that *Playboy* was a lifestyle magazine for young men that offered a glimpse into a fantasy world which was actually attainable. His goal after the initial success of *Playboy* was to retool the magazine from its initial form as a handmade rag put together on a table in his apartment to a quality-driven, forward-thinking periodical representative of the liberal, modern men of the post-war era. In short, Hugh Hefner hoped to produce an intellectual magazine that would directly affect society's views on sex and self-gratification. He wanted society to leave its repressive sexual thinking behind and instead, embrace a new freedom and focus on making its people happy, fulfilled, and satisfied.

ONE PART RISK, ONE PART BELIEF, AND ONE PART GOOD LUCK

Throughout his lifetime, Hugh Hefner has made it clear that he realizes he was in the right place at the right time when he launched *Playboy*, but more importantly, he realized in 1953 that his inner monologue and discordant thinking wasn't nonconformist at all. Instead, men from across the United States felt exactly the same way that the young Hugh Hefner did, and *Playboy* gave those feelings legitimacy. The timing was right for *Playboy*, which launched after the dark years of the Great Depression, World War I, and World War II. The 1950s represented a shift in thinking from external to internal. Rather than focusing on wars overseas, Americans found themselves with time to think about their own happiness. The prosperous post-war years also gave people access to discretionary incomes they hadn't known before. A magazine like *Playboy*, which celebrated a lifestyle consumed with personal gratification and self-fulfillment, was positioned perfectly in the 1950s.

Playboy in the 1950s was viewed by many as a rebellious, inappropriate magazine that represented little more than a hedonistic lifestyle, but to many more, it represented an alternate way of thinking than the established norm. That way of thinking was one that more people, particularly the members of the twenty-something Silent Generation (see Box 2.1 for more information about the Silent Generation), aspired to embrace than anyone could have expected. The magazine offered an opportunity for people to live and think in a different way, and *Playboy* told them there was nothing wrong with them for living and thinking this way. At its core, *Playboy* fulfilled an existing need in the marketplace. It's a fundamental business truth that creating a product to fulfill an existing need is far easier than creating a perceived need to fulfill the business objectives of an existing product. The interesting point for *Playboy* was that in the closed-door social environment of the 1950s, no one realized just how big that need and the corresponding marketplace actually was until the magazine debuted.

REINVENTING AN INDUSTRY—THE YEARS UP TO 1959

> **BOX 2.1   The Silent Generation**
>
> The Silent Generation was made up of individuals born between the years of 1925–1945, between World War I and World War II. Hugh Hefner was a member of this generation, although he was born on the cusp of the previous G.I. Generation and the Silent Generation.
>
> Members of the Silent Generation were considered to be cautious and withdrawn, primarily because they were confused by a widely shared internal struggle between existing morals and lifestyles, and their own ideas and desires (demonstrating that there was an audience waiting for a product and brand like Playboy). While most members of this generation remained silent (as the name implies), some did have the courage to take the initiative and speak out against the political, religious, and social norms they questioned. Hugh Hefner was one of those people who chose action over acceptance.

Within one year, *Playboy* was selling 185,000 copies per month, and by the end of 1959, circulation had jumped to 1.1 million copies per month—more than *Esquire*. *Playboy* was enjoying an unprecedented success stemming from Hugh Hefner's $8,000 investment. To give the success of *Playboy* perspective, consider that *Time* magazine launched *Sports Illustrated* around the same time that *Playboy* debuted not only with much success but also with a much larger budget—an estimated $30 million.

But what was the secret to *Playboy*'s early success? It could be argued that *Playboy* succeeded initially for three primary reasons:

1. *Playboy* fulfilled an existing need among consumers.
2. *Playboy* was different from any other product in the marketplace.
3. *Playboy* targeted a specific niche audience.

As discussed earlier in this chapter, *Playboy* met the fundamental business truth that creating a product to fulfill an existing customer need is far easier than creating a perceived need to fulfill the business objectives of an existing product. *Playboy* took the category of men's magazines dominated by *Esquire* in the 1950s a step further and created a unique product that appealed to a very specific consumer segment. In fact, the first issue of *Playboy* stated whom the magazine was intended for and ordered people outside of that consumer segment to pass it on to the type of person it was meant for.

A BRAND IS BORN

An introduction in the first issue of *Playboy* read, "If you're a man between the ages of 18 and 80, *Playboy* is meant for you. If you like your entertainment served up with humor, sophistication and spice, *Playboy* will become a very special favorite. We want to make it clear from the very start, we aren't a 'family magazine.' If you're somebody's sister, wife, or mother-in-law and picked us up by mistake, please pass us along to the man in your life and get back to your *Ladies Home Companion*." The introduction went on to tell readers exactly what they could expect from *Playboy* magazine, "We plan on spending most of our time inside. We like our apartment. We enjoy mixing up cocktails and an hors d'oeuvre or two, putting a little mood music on the phonograph, and inviting in a female acquaintance for a quiet discussion on Picasso, Nietzsche, jazz, sex. Affairs of the state will be out of our province."

From the start, the target audience was defined and consumer expectations were set. Luckily for Hugh Hefner, his instincts about *Playboy* were accurate, and consumers pulled their hard-earned money out of their wallets to buy it. Interestingly, *Playboy*'s success didn't come from years of market research, demographic analyses, and behavioral modeling. Instead, it came as a result of one man's instinct that there were more people in the United States who thought the way he did and would like to join together in sharing those thoughts through a new magazine. Hefner has admitted he based many of his early business decisions on instinct rather than traditional business acumen. It's a risk (with a bit of luck) that paid off very well.

EARLY PROMOTION TACTICS

Hugh Hefner's goal was never to create a sex magazine but rather a lifestyle magazine that included elements of sex. He viewed *Playboy* as a complete entertainment package that provided useful, quality content which young men could actually use to live the fantasy depicted on the pages in their own lives. It's the lifestyle Hugh Hefner wanted, and it turned out, it was a lifestyle many men aspired to lead. With his goal of creating a quality literary magazine at the core of everything he did for *Playboy* in the early years, Hefner sought to create content that was better than what people found in *Esquire* and other men's magazines. He focused on creating a magazine that included a mix of articles, humor, interviews, and pictorials all with a tasteful theme. What made *Playboy* emerge early on as a publishing pioneer was its use of marketing promotion tactics to drive awareness, attract attention, develop customer expectations, and earn customer loyalty.

The marketing push started with Hugh Hefner's coup in obtaining nude photos of Marilyn Monroe to appear in the first issue of *Playboy*. The public heard about the possible existence of these photos long before December 1953, but Hugh Hefner took the initiative to find them, recognizing their potential as bait to drive awareness of his magazine. With only $8,000 to launch *Playboy*, there was no money in the budget for publicity or promotion. Scoring the nude Marilyn Monroe photos was a significant accomplishment that helped drive initial sales and consumer buzz about *Playboy* more than Hefner could have hoped.

The initial buzz about the nude Marilyn Monroe photos was followed with tease marketing tactics. A clothed-Marilyn Monroe graced the cover of the first issue of *Playboy* but teaser copy on the cover told all who took a cursory glance at the new magazine sitting on the newsstand shelf that inside were "full-color" nude photos of Monroe. Certainly, more than one passerby was moved to action and purchased the first issue of *Playboy* based on that promise. However, the promise went a step further. The teaser copy made it clear that full-color nude photos of beautiful women would appear "in every issue." With just a few words of well-written and well-positioned copy, customer expectations were set. Hefner's initial bait-and-hook method worked. Next, he had to create a customer experience that would allow consumers to become emotionally involved in the Playboy brand, so they would keep coming back again and again. He would achieve that goal with quality content.

The content of *Playboy* magazine was fairly consistent from one issue to the next with regular features included in every issue. Again, consumer expectations were set and met month after month. The first issue of *Playboy* introduced the Sweetheart of the Month (renamed Playmate of the Month in the second issue), a feature that continued to run over five decades later. Cartoons, fiction, interviews, and more were staples in every *Playboy* magazine. The consistency from one issue to the next represented a critical step in building a strong brand. The young Hugh Hefner had no idea he was in the process of creating an iconic brand at the time. He was simply going by his own instincts and creating a magazine that was representative of the life he wanted to live.

Hefner controlled all aspects of the magazine in the early days, from the writing to the photos, art to everything in between. *Playboy* truly was one man's vision, but it was a vision that many men wanted to share. While other men's magazines focused on sports and "masculine" activities with women completely removed from the picture, *Playboy* did exactly the opposite. It focused completely on women and the relationship between men and women. Rather than telling readers to go out and drink beers with the guys and go hunting, *Playboy* told readers to put on jazz music, make a gourmet dinner, and drink fine wine with a beautiful woman. It's a change consumers wanted and accepted fully. The proof was in *Playboy*'s rising circulation numbers.

Buoyed by the early success of *Playboy*, Hugh Hefner continued to reinvest the profits he earned back into the magazine and set even higher goals for *Playboy*. Rather than simply being a men's lifestyle magazine, *Playboy* came to represent Hefner's goal to change society's views on sex and self-gratification. In essence, the magazine's "philosophy" grew with Hefner's evolving personal views (see Chapter 6 for more information on the Playboy Philosophy). As the 1950s passed, *Playboy* grew in terms of audience size, sales, profits, and its vision.

At first, Hefner used models and public domain articles to fill the pages of *Playboy*, but within a short time, he began looking for women with a "girl next door" look who had no modeling experience. The use of average but beautiful women added to the allure of the *Playboy* fantasy lifestyle. It created additional expectations among readers who came to believe that this lifestyle they read about in the pages of *Playboy* was truly attainable. It brought a sense of personalization to *Playboy* as readers associated the women in *Playboy* pictorials to people they could actually meet.

When biographies were added to the Playmate of the Month feature outlining each Playmate's interests, hobbies, activities, and so on, readers could personalize the magazine's content even more. Readers felt like they knew the women on the pages of the magazine and they could count on *Playboy* to deliver on their expectations month after month. The rest of the pages of *Playboy* in the 1950s were dedicated to showing readers how to live the Playboy lifestyle. Articles about clothes, music, food, and even consumer products demonstrated how readers could (and should) spend the money they had during the prosperous 1950s on treating themselves to the lifestyle they desired and deserved. From the beginning, *Playboy* represented a perfectly executed relationship brand. *Playboy* delivered on the brand's promise of helping young men reinvent themselves to achieve personal satisfaction and freedom month after month, and readership continued to grow as consumers personalized the material in the magazine and integrated

> **BOX 2.2** Understanding relationship branding
>
> A relationship brand is one based on shared customer experiences with a brand. The brand has mass appeal but each individual consumer is given the opportunity to experience the brand in their own way, which allows them to develop a personal connection with the brand and become emotionally involved with it.
>
> Successful relationship brands are ones where customers are in control. They are given the opportunity to self-select their experiences with the brand. The company behind the brand must deliver products and services that appeal to different customer segments within the overall audience with the understanding that consumers within those varied segments will have different wants and needs from the brand.

it into their own fantasies and lives. The recipe for a successful relationship brand was in place from the beginning (see Box 2.2 for more information about relationship branding).

The Playboy brand offered value to various consumer segments through articles, humor, pictorials, and more. Readers could choose which features they related to and control their own experiences with the brand. As the lifecycle of the Playboy brand progressed, new brand extensions provided ways for a broader consumer audience to experience the brand and build relationships with it.

Another example of a relationship brand is Apple. In the early days of the Apple brand lifecycle, it developed a reputation as a cult brand, which appealed only to a tight-knit group of designers. Over time, Apple expanded its product offerings to develop a broader reach and appeal. By the mid-2000s, Apple was one of the most successful relationship brands on the market. Consumers believed the Apple brand promise and were willing to spend more on Apple products because they felt emotionally connected to it.

Apple took its quest to become a relationship brand seriously. The company created branded experiences such as Apple Stores and developed products that organically called for sharing and personal connection. Consumers felt secure in the Apple brand, which always delivered on its consistent brand promise. Furthermore, consumers felt valued and as a result, professed their loyalty to Apple both financially and vocally by buying Apple products and advocating them to friends, family, and anyone who would listen.

In the 1950s, *Playboy* positioned itself well for ongoing sales boosts by convincing famous women looking for their own publicity to allow their photos to be published in *Playboy* magazine. Famous women used *Playboy* to draw attention to their careers. It worked, and it's a practice that women still use today, over half a century later. For example, Pamela Anderson attributes much of her success to her appearances in *Playboy* magazine. With each big name star that posed for *Playboy* came an opportunity for promotion that Hefner leveraged fully. Not only did celebrities bring short-term attention to *Playboy*, but over time, the association of celebrities with *Playboy* would give the brand even more legitimacy and power and brought Hefner closer to the Hollywood lifestyle he idolized since childhood.

Playboy's primary customers in the 1950s were college-educated, professional men. They worked hard, earned money, and wanted to spend it on themselves to live a good life. *Playboy* made them feel like there was nothing wrong with those desires, and in fact, promoted them. *Playboy* told consumers who had long heard that self-denial was the only way to live, that it was time to change the rules. The magazine interspersed a fantasy lifestyle with articles and features relevant to young men living in the post-war era, and consumers responded strongly. For Hugh Hefner, *Playboy* was to be a leader, not a follower, and that was evident from the debut issue in December 1953. The publishing world would never be the same and an iconic brand had been born.

CHAPTER 3

NURTURING A BRAND

[Playboy] tried to personalize the concept of pin-up photography.
Hugh Hefner, 1983 Interview with
Greg Jackson of ABC News

The early days of the Playboy brand did not come without challenges. From the beginning, Hugh Hefner faced roadblocks from the facets of society that found the content of *Playboy* offensive. However, he also met obstacles from sources like the U.S. Postal Service, the police, and the FBI. The 1950s marked the birth of a brand that would take the world by storm and cause social and business changes that no one could have expected.

While Hugh Hefner hoped to liberate thinking about sex and self-gratification, not everyone was ready for the change he advocated. To these people, the Playboy brand represented everything that was wrong with the world—people turning their backs on established norms and values. To Hugh Hefner and the early fans of *Playboy*, the early days of the sexual revolution were underway, and there was no turning back. *Playboy* was originally targeted to a niche of college-educated professionals but quickly grew to include an audience of young men who wanted to achieve the lifestyle displayed on the pages of *Playboy* and needed direction to find the path to nirvana. Readers believed in the Playboy brand promise and the change Hefner advocated and fought for despite the negative backlash he and Playboy faced.

UNDERSTANDING THE ENVIRONMENT IN THE 1950s

An important aspect of marketing a new product is in understanding the environment that product will have to perform in. As discussed in Chapter 2, Hugh Hefner spent no time pondering the current or future environments when he launched *Playboy*, but an analysis of the environment in the 1950s is essential to understand the early challenges and opportunities the Playboy brand faced. Truth be told, a thorough market evaluation in the early 1950s probably would have told Hugh Hefner that starting *Playboy* was not a wise investment. For that reason, his entrepreneurial genius attributed significantly to his success. Without his reliance on instinct and willingness to take a blind risk, he may not have created one of the most iconic brands of the 20th century. With that in mind, high-level reviews of the macro and micro environments of the early 1950s follow.

The Macro Environment in the 1950s

The macro environment includes the political, economic, societal, and technological factors influencing the world at a given point in time. In the 1950s, politics were conservative. The world had recently emerged from World War II, and the government still controlled many aspects of life that repressed personal freedom, particularly the right to free speech and equality. This repressive political agenda fueled Hugh Hefner's drive to increase personal freedoms.

On the economic front, people had more disposable income than ever, and they wanted to spend it. In Hugh Hefner's mind, it was time for men to start spending money on themselves and living the good life they would learn about within the pages of his magazine. The majority of society, however, was not prepared for the lifestyle Hugh Hefner proposed. Religion and family values still dominated thinking in the 1950s, despite the fact that many people lived closer to the Playboy lifestyle behind closed doors than they were willing to admit. It was this hypocrisy that spurred Hugh Hefner to push the envelope and convince people that it was time to open those doors and live freely.

Finally, technology played a role in the early 1950s. More families had access to information than ever before through expanding television, movies, transportation, and more. The Playboy lifestyle welcomed these technological influences, and faster moving publicity generated a strong buzz around the brand early on. In short, the macro environment was open to the emergence of *Playboy* and the lifestyle and freedoms it advocated, but a closer analysis would show that the political and societal aspects of that environment may not be prepared to make the big leap *Playboy* urged.

The Micro Environment in the 1950s

The micro environment (or internal forces at work) within HMH Publishing in the early 1950s was another story entirely. This was an area of the Playboy brand strategy that Hugh Hefner could control, and control it he did. All aspects of *Playboy* were created by, reviewed by, or approved by Hugh Hefner. He hired a team of workers in the 1950s that believed in *Playboy* and fully supported the brand. However, at all times, employees were completely aware of who was in control—Hugh Hefner. That's not to say that *Playboy* didn't have to overcome obstacles presented by the micro environment in the 1950s. On more than one occasion local backlash from the Chicago community that Hefner depended on presented challenges for *Playboy*, and a lost line of credit in 1956 could have ended the company. However, Hefner faced each challenge head-on, even going to the length of giving up his own salary and 25% of his company stock when the bank pulled the aforementioned line of credit, in order to ensure that *Playboy* succeeded.

KEEPING UP WITH BRAND GROWTH

In 1954, Hugh Hefner moved his work out of his home and into a Chicago office. He quickly realized that his men's lifestyle magazine was growing in popularity fast, and he needed help. He hired assistants and eventually an editorial staff to keep up with the unprecedented growth of *Playboy* but still retained decision-making authority in all aspects of the business. Hefner also recognized the need to work with people who were known in the publishing industry in order to give the brand a boost in terms of respectability. His new staff helped him not only to get the day-to-day work done but also to make new contacts, find better, well-known writers, and take advantage of opportunities to extend the brand into new markets. His new staff also gave him time to fight the battles *Playboy* would face throughout its lifecycle but particularly in the 1950s when it was gaining momentum.

One of the first big hurdles *Playboy* had to overcome to continue on its growth trajectory was presented at the hands of the U.S. Postal Service. In the early 1950s, sending items through the mail that included photographs of nude women was considered obscene, and the U.S. Post Office deemed *Playboy* to be exactly that. As a result, the Post Office denied a request for *Playboy* to be granted a second class mail permit, which all periodicals used at the time. Hugh Hefner faced the battle head-on. HMH Publishing sued and won the right to use second class mail privileges as well as $100,000 in compensation. It was the first of many court battles Hugh Hefner would face during the lifecycle of the Playboy brand.

The year 1954 also presented *Playboy* with obstacles from the conservative majority who initiated bans throughout the country against *Playboy*. The magazine was banned in bookstores, city suburbs, and colleges, but each banning simply fueled the buzz around the Playboy brand. At the same time, a public relations firm was successfully getting the *Playboy* name into newspapers and Hugh Hefner was booked for interviews and television shows, including high-profile programs. There was always something to talk about with regards to the Playboy brand in the 1950s, and the public wanted to hear more about it with each new piece of information that was released.

At a time when communications were slower than people are accustomed to in the 21st century, Americans were insatiably intrigued with *Playboy* and the man who quickly became the face of *Playboy*. Whether people approved or disapproved of *Playboy*, they wanted to hear more about the magazine and the man behind the brand. It's a position Hefner would embrace more fully as the decade came to an end. When the FBI began investigating Hefner in 1957 due to his liberal views about sex, his position as the Playboy brand ambassador and agent of change was solidified not just by consumers and society but also by the U.S. government.

Despite the controversy surrounding *Playboy* during its infancy, advertisers were attracted to it. In 1956, Springmaid became the first major brand to advertise in *Playboy*, and other brands were quick to follow, particularly after a 1958 research study by Daniel Starch & Staff reported that *Playboy* readers were an average age of 28 (a coveted audience) and spent more overall, as well as within a variety of specific categories, than any other magazine readers (of the 50 magazines included in the study). Suddenly, advertising in *Playboy* took on a new significance and represented a sizeable opportunity.

As the Playboy brand grew, Hugh Hefner's belief in the product he created also grew causing him not only to work at a feverish pace to produce and market his magazine but also to form a false sense of power as the face of the Playboy brand. As it turned out, the magazine's popularity grew enough to support that false sense of power and actually allowed the brand to explode even further in popularity. Hugh Hefner would become the ultimate brand champion as the face of the brand and symbol of the lifestyle *Playboy* represented.

HUGH HEFNER REINVENTS HIMSELF AGAIN AND THE ULTIMATE BRAND CHAMPION ARRIVES

As the 1950s passed, Hugh Hefner found himself quickly becoming the central figure of *Playboy*. From the business perspective, editorial side, and public image, Hefner was the face of the Playboy brand. It's not entirely surprising that he would begin to live the lifestyle he so vocally advocated within the pages of *Playboy* magazine. In 1957, Hefner officially separated from his first wife after years of marital struggles. It wasn't until March 1959 that the divorce was finalized, but that didn't stop Hefner from becoming the ultimate brand champion not just with his words but also with his actions. The changes Hefner made in his lifestyle in the late 1950s would set the stage for an explosion in Playboy brand popularity in the 1960s.

While some of the habits that formed the Hugh Hefner persona that followed him throughout his life began organically and quite separate from his attempt to become a Playboy himself (e.g., he began working in his pajamas day and night as a result of his workaholic personality as early as 1954), it was during the late 1950s that Hugh Hefner made the conscious decision to live the Playboy lifestyle. He recognized the power of celebrity, which he had long been obsessed with, and worked to leverage that power. Marking the second reinvention of Hugh Hefner at the time of his separation from his first wife, Hefner presented himself to the world in the June 1957 issue of *Playboy* as the physical embodiment of the Playboy lifestyle. With his new penchants for pipe smoking and dating multiple women, the world became even more intrigued with Hefner and *Playboy*. Hefner fed the world's insatiable appetites by appearing in public more often, partying at night, and showing people how wonderful the Playboy lifestyle could be. As the decade wore on, he became the symbol of self-gratification, materialism, and sexual freedom—mirroring the Playboy brand promise.

In the 1950s, the Playboy lifestyle was alive and well, not just for Hugh Hefner, but also for the people who worked for him. Nowhere was the Playboy lifestyle more fully advocated than within the walls of the *Playboy* offices in Chicago. With the ultimate brand champion setting the example, employees were quick to adapt the lifestyle as well, making them strong brand ambassadors and thereby attaining every brand manager's ultimate goal of developing internal brand advocates who worked tirelessly to defend the brand, praise the brand, and grow the brand. There are few things more influential than employee brand advocates. Within the confines of the *Playboy* offices, life was good, employees were loyal, and they loved *Playboy*. That combination can be infinitely powerful in terms of brand success.

It's important to note, however, that despite the free lifestyle and public persona Hugh Hefner represented in the late 1950s, he never lost sight of his primary goal—publishing a literary magazine for young men. It was his actions as brand champion that helped catapult it to early success despite the challenges it faced and allowed it to develop into a powerful brand faster than any other product, particularly within the publishing market. Hugh Hefner wasn't a businessman, but he was a man who believed in his product completely. His passion was contagious and everyone around him caught the *Playboy* bug (or infection as the case may be).

The next phase of the Playboy brand lifecycle would come in the form of a series of early brand extensions that defied business logic but succeeded in making the brand even more powerful. It seemed that anything Hugh Hefner touched in association with the Playboy brand turned to gold despite the controversy that consistently surrounded the brand. *Playboy* is the perfect example of how something that is forbidden or deemed inappropriate becomes more desirable than it may have been without the negative publicity surrounding it. Curiosity leads to brand buzz and sales. For *Playboy*, it led to fast success beyond anyone's imagination.

CHAPTER 4

THE FIRST BRAND EXTENSIONS

> *The business aspects of the company never really interested me as long as we had the money to do the things I wanted to do. For me, the magazine was always the heart of what my life was all about, and the other half was living the life.*
>
> Hugh Hefner, December 2008 Interview with Askmen.com

While traditional marketing plans typically call for allowing a brand to grow and attain a stronghold within its market before extending that brand into new categories, in the 1950s, Hugh Hefner had no knowledge of how traditional marketing plans worked. When he saw opportunities to extend the Playboy brand, he seized them. It could be argued that this was a direct result of his undaunting view of the Playboy lifestyle and *Playboy* magazine. However, he did follow some of the rules of branding by ensuring that each brand extension accurately represented the Playboy image and promise. In essence, Hefner was following the three primary steps of branding from the moment Playboy was born.

The three primary steps of branding are

1. *Definition*: Define the desired image the brand will portray in the marketplace.
2. *Communication*: Communicate the brand message.
3. *Persistence and consistency*: Be consistent and persistent with the brand message and image.

THE FIRST BRAND EXTENSIONS

The Playboy brand was defined from day one. There was no doubt where it would be positioned in the marketplace, what its image would be, and what its primary message would be. This was a magazine for young men that celebrated a sexually liberated lifestyle focused on self-gratification. There was nothing else quite like it on the market. Communicating the brand message was done directly through the pages of *Playboy* magazine. The introduction printed in the first pages of the debut issue of *Playboy* magazine (see Chapter 2 for an excerpt of the introduction) made it very clear whom the intended audience was and what the magazine would deliver. The brand message, image, and promise were succinctly communicated in the magazine as well as through the living Playboy, Hugh Hefner, via interviews, public appearances, court battles, and so on.

The third key step in branding is persistence and consistency. This is where Hugh Hefner unknowingly made decisions that would protect *Playboy* and its brand image and message. Inconsistent branding leads to consumer confusion, but consistent branding is essential to create customer expectations for a brand, which leads to brand loyalty. When the brand promise is met again and again, consumers feel a sense of security in that brand and develop a strong loyalty to it. Over time, they become emotionally involved in that brand and their loyalty deepens to the point where they become brand advocates and influencers. Brand loyalty is the ultimate goal when any new brand is launched.

Whether or not Hugh Hefner realized he was building brand value by ensuring the Playboy brand communicated a consistent image and message to consumers is unknown, but the fact that he vigilantly controlled all aspects of the brand with extremely high standards, led to successful, consistent branding. For example, Hefner would not accept ads in *Playboy* that did not fit the brand, regardless of the amount of money an ad could generate. Furthermore, no content could be published on the pages of *Playboy* that was not consistent with the Playboy brand. And just as a company creates corporate identity standards, Hefner created a "basic editorial attitude" for *Playboy*, which included rules related to type, punctuation, proofreading, style, and so on. He held final approval on everything that appeared in the magazine, from art to photos, articles, and more. If content didn't meet Hefner's exacting standards for *Playboy* it wasn't included. All content had to push the envelope in terms of advocating sexual freedom while remaining in good taste at the same time. The goal of the Playboy brand was always to maintain its position as a quality magazine for young men.

To attain brand loyalty, consistency *and* persistence are needed. In other words, messages must be consistent, but they also have to be continual. Consumers are fickle and forget a brand quickly. Without brand persistence, consumers will move onto the next big thing with nary a backward glance. While typically marketing plans tell brand managers to build that persistent message through advertising and promotions, Playboy benefited from publicity as well as an unprecedented series of brand extensions in the 1950s, which kept the brand top of mind and in the spotlight for years to come.

PLAYBOY DEFIES MARKETING RULES

There are established rules to brand extensions that marketers tend to accept and follow, but for Hugh Hefner and Playboy, there were no rules. Instead, a rogue mentality evolved where the powerful Playboy brand was positioned to grow faster than traditional marketing plans would ever recommend. To get a better idea of how the extension of the Playboy brand went against the marketing status quo, consider the most basic conditions marketers typically evaluate before investing in brand extensions:

1. Assess the new category and the parent brand's position and acceptance within that category.
2. Assess the impact of the extension on the parent brand.

It could be argued that Hugh Hefner bypassed Step 1 completely. Luckily, most of the early Playboy brand extensions were accepted by consumers within each new category the brand entered (however, not without the controversy that always followed the brand and fueled the buzz), but certainly, no brand extension was entered into lightly when it came to assessing the impact on the parent brand. For Hugh Hefner, no brand extension could negatively impact the quality of the Playboy brand. He managed brand extensions exactly the same way that he managed the content of *Playboy* magazine—each had to accurately reflect the lifestyle that the brand promised.

It didn't take long for Hugh Hefner to find ways to extend the Playboy brand. Was it his genius entrepreneurial spirit or dumb luck that made it work? That's up for debate, but the point is—it worked. By 1957, the Playboy brand had extended into merchandising with items such as clothing, jewelry, bar accessories, playing cards, and more;

THE FIRST BRAND EXTENSIONS

all available with the Playboy logo emblazoned on them. Hefner also extended the Playboy brand into several books in the 1950s such as *Playboy's Party Jokes*.

As the 1950s drew to a close, Hugh Hefner launched several brand extensions that would truly bring the Playboy brand to the next level of success. First, he purchased the Chicago Playboy Mansion. His new home was huge and equally large in terms of representing the Playboy lifestyle he so vocally advocated. Stories of parties and activities that happened at the Chicago Playboy Mansion would become fodder for men's fantasies across the country as Hugh Hefner took the idea of the Playboy lifestyle to the most extreme level of self-indulgence, materialism, and personal freedom. The ultimate brand champion became an even bigger celebrity, and the press and buzz surrounding the Playboy brand grew exponentially. By the end of 1959, circulation of *Playboy* magazine reached over 1 million copies and had long surpassed *Esquire* as the most popular men's magazine. In fact, *Playboy* had become one of the largest selling magazines in the United States with no signs of losing ground anytime soon.

That kind of success makes it difficult to resist extending the brand, particularly a relationship brand like Playboy that is so deeply rooted in personalization and experience. For Hugh Hefner, the brand needed to take on a new form where consumers could actually experience the lifestyle the brand promised. With that goal in mind, the concept of the Playboy Club was created as another touch point where consumers could experience and personalize the brand (the first Playboy Club would open in February 1960). But first, a television show that depicted the Playboy lifestyle would debut in October 1959 called *Playboy's Penthouse*.

The program was based on a cocktail party atmosphere at a real-life Playboy's apartment. Hugh Hefner played the role of the Playboy as he hosted celebrity guests such as Sammy Davis Jr., Tony Bennett, and more with the goal of consistently extending the Playboy brand while attracting national advertisers for the magazine at the same time. According to Hefner, "I was using *Playboy's Penthouse* as a promotional vehicle that made *Playboy* real," (*Playboy 2000: The Party Continues*). *Playboy's Penthouse* was syndicated to twelve cities and lasted for two seasons. While the show itself wasn't going to win any awards, it did successfully bring another aspect of the Playboy lifestyle into people's homes allowing them to experience it, personalize it, and develop deeper relationships with it, which made the fantasy seem attainable and drove additional interest in the lifestyle, the brand, and the magazine (see Box 4.1 for more information about experience brands).

BOX 4.1 Defining an experience brand

An experience brand is one that engages a consumer, rather than simply delivering a means to an end. Experience brands often surround consumers and integrate with the physical world around them. By offering ways for consumers to experience a brand's promise, consumers can personally connect with it and develop relationships with it. That connection becomes more powerful when consumers can share those experiences with others. As early as the 1950s, Playboy offered consumers a variety of ways to experience the brand through *Playboy* magazine, the Playboy Jazz Festival, television, Playboy Clubs, and more.

Another example of an experience brand was Saturn in the early 1990s when it first debuted. At the time, Saturn was advertised as "a different kind of car company" where consumers would find a completely different car buying experience than they had ever seen before. There would be no price haggling or hidden fees. The days of the "hard-sell" were over and customers were treated like friends. Waiting rooms looked like living rooms, complete with couches and televisions, and the service department always went the extra mile, often at no extra charge.

The Saturn way was a breath of fresh air and consumers loved it. They formed Saturn owners clubs and vocally spoke of the wonders of their local dealership, the company, and the brand. The Saturn cars were nothing amazing, but the Saturn experience was.

Disney is another example of a powerful experience brand. Today, consumers can find a wide variety of immersive Disney-branded experiences, including theme parks, television shows, merchandise, magazines, music, radio stations, stores, Web sites, cruise ships, island destinations, and more. Consumers become highly emotionally involved with the Disney brand, and they are given the opportunity to self-select the experiences they want to share with the brand and with other people.

Disney-branded experiences are consistent and continual. There is no doubt in the minds of consumers that they are experiencing the Disney brand when they visit a Disney theme park, Disney store, or Disney Web site. In fact, to ensure the brand is portrayed consistently, the Walt Disney Company has created separate brands for projects and businesses that don't accurately reflect the Disney brand. For example, the Touchstone brand name is attached to

THE FIRST BRAND EXTENSIONS

> Disney-produced films that the company believes are not in-line with the family-friendly Disney brand so as not to confuse consumers about the focused Disney brand message—family-friendly entertainment. In other words, consumers have expectations for the Disney brand, and the Walt Disney Company understands those expectations and the need to deliver on the Disney brand promise at all times.

Another Playboy brand experience debuted in August 1959 when the first Playboy Jazz Festival was held at Chicago Stadium (after being moved from Soldier Field following protests by the Roman Catholic Church) and featured celebrity performances by Dizzy Gillespie, Miles Davis, Louis Armstrong, and more. The crowd surpassed 18,000 people, and when Playboy donated all profits to Chicago's Urban League, the brand was positioned as more than just a hedonistic magazine. It was an integral part of the Chicago culture. Furthermore, Playboy Tours, a line of jazz albums, and the Playboy Modeling Agency were launched as additional brand extensions with the goal of furthering the brand as a complete entertainment package along with the brand message of enjoying life.

In the latter half of the 1950s, the Playboy brand was available to people to experience in multiple formats. In other words, consumers were given choices and were able to take control of how they would experience the brand and make it their own thereby personalizing it. At the same time, the various extensions provided opportunities for consumers to share the brand experience. Watching *Playboy's Penthouse* together or attending the Playboy Jazz Festival gave people multiple ways to experience the brand, making it not just a relationship brand, but a societal brand where groups of people could share their experiences with the brand together. At the same time, Playboy became a deeply emotional brand as consumers developed both shared and personal connections with it (see Box 4.2 for more information about consumer emotional involvement theory). Regardless of how consumers wanted to interact with the brand, they were given options early on in the brand lifecycle and allowed to take control of their experiences. Again, without realizing it, Hugh Hefner was making wise, branding decisions.

The four orders of brand experience can be directly applied to the success of the Playboy brand. From the early days of the Playboy brand's rise to success, brand extensions gave consumers different

> **BOX 4.2 Consumer emotional involvement theory**
>
> As consumers experience a brand and begin to believe in that brand's promise, they will develop an emotional attachment to it. A primary goal of brand building is developing customer loyalty, which comes directly from activities that drive emotional involvement—consistently and persistently delivering your brand message and meeting customer expectations for the brand.
>
> Over time, a consumer's emotional involvement with a brand grows deeper and evolves into a strong personal connection to that brand, which drives them to repurchase the brand, advocate the brand, and protect the brand. In other words, emotionally involved consumers are the most effective brand ambassadors.
>
> Consider a brand like Starbucks that spent the majority of the early 2000s creating consumer emotional involvement in the brand. It's hard to imagine 10 years earlier that people would one day be willing to pay $7 for a cup of coffee that they could get elsewhere for one-quarter of that price, but by the 2000s, they did. In fact, consumers would drive far and wide for their mocha lattes. Starbucks sold more than a cup of coffee. The brand represented a better coffee buying and coffee drinking experience. Suddenly, a cup of Dunkin' Donuts coffee wasn't good enough. Starbucks offered so much more for emotionally attached consumers. Even when the economy weakened in the United States in the late 2000s, many loyal Starbucks consumers still could not live without their Starbucks and continued to pay exorbitant prices for their beloved brand.

ways to experience the brand and the lifestyle the brand promise represented. Taking a look at the four orders of brand experience in Figure 4.1, there are four levels of experience that a consumer can participate in with a brand. These experiences range from passive participation to active participation and between these two extremes consumers either experience the brand on a superficial or immersive level.

For example, a Playboy consumer in Level 1 of the four orders of brand experience, the Quaternary level, passively and superficially experiences a brand. That person might watch *Playboy's Penthouse* on television simply absorbing the sights and sounds but doing little else. A Playboy consumer in Level 2 of the four orders of brand experience, the Tertiary level, passively and immersively experiences the brand.

THE FIRST BRAND EXTENSIONS

Level 4
Quaternary level
Active-engrossed experience
Consumers actively and immersively experience a brand.

Level 3
Tertiary level
Active-peripheral experience
Consumers actively and superficially experience a brand.

Level 2
Secondary level
Passive-engrossed experience
Consumers passively and immersively experience a brand.

Level 1
Primary level
Passive-peripheral experience
Consumers passively and superficially experience a brand.

Active experiences
Passive experiences

Level of brand experience

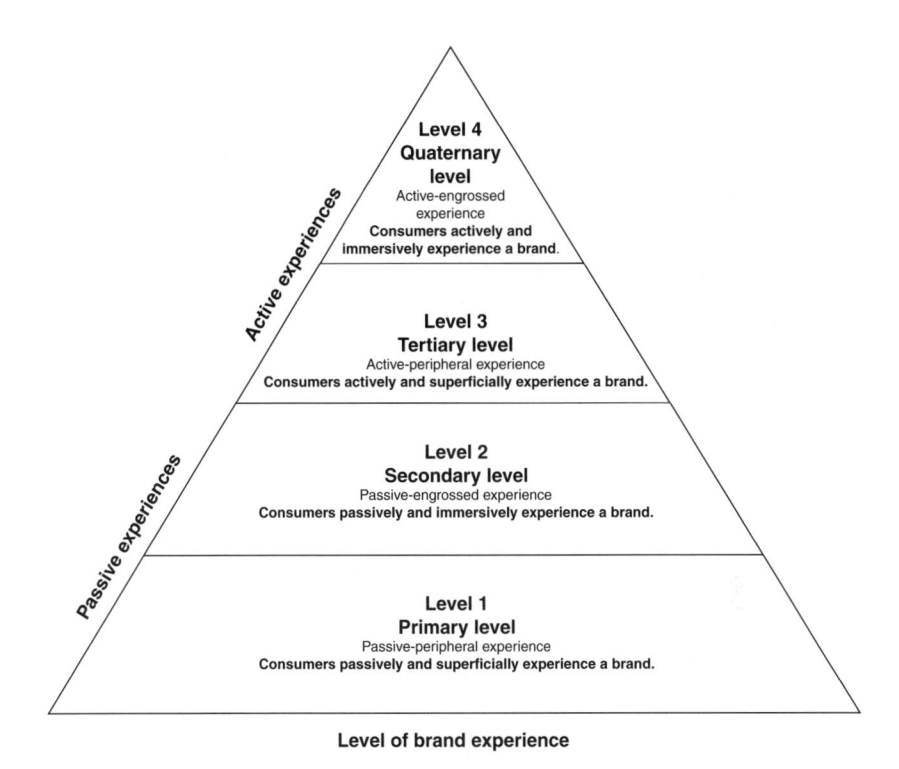

FIGURE 4.1 **Four orders of brand experience**

That person might attend a Playboy Jazz Festival simply to be a part of the immersive experience. He or she simply watches and listens passively but the brand is surrounding them as part of the experience. A Playboy consumer in Level 3 of the Four orders of brand experience, the Secondary level, actively and superficially experiences the brand. For example, that person might read *Playboy* magazine and actively try to learn from the content and apply the information to his own life to attain the fantasy lifestyle the brand promises, but he is not immersed in the brand experience. Playboy consumers in Level 4 of the Four orders of brand experience, the Primary level, are actively participating and completely immersed in the brand experience. A patron to the Playboy Club in Las Vegas is a perfect example of a Playboy consumer experiencing the brand in Level 4 of the Four orders of brand experience.

The take-away is this—as early as the 1950s, Playboy was already positioned to become a powerful brand. It had all the elements a power brand could possibly want and more, such as:

- Consumer buzz
- Publicity
- Differentiation
- Various touch-points or experience realms
- A visible brand champion
- Strong employee brand advocates
- A clear brand image, message, and promise
- Consistency in setting and meeting customer expectations
- Restraint in protecting the brand
- An untapped niche

While it certainly goes against tested marketing theory to extend a brand so much and so quickly, it worked for Playboy. Of course, the risk with quick, successive brand extensions is that the market will become saturated with the brand and the brand will become diluted in consumers' minds. However, that was not the case with Playboy, at least not at first. It would take years for the Playboy brand and the people behind it to realize that there is such a thing as the need for focus and contraction to maximize returns, but in the 1950s, life was good, the brand was strong, and all signs pointed to continued success.

PART II
A BRAND RISES DESPITE THE NAYSAYERS—THE 1960s

TABLE II **Timeline—The 1960s**

1960: The first Playboy Club opens in Chicago. Hugh Hefner creates the Playboy Advisor.

1961: Comic Dick Gregory performs at the Chicago Playboy Club becoming the first African American performer to appear in a mainstream nightclub.

1962: The Playboy Philosophy and the Playboy Interview debut in *Playboy* magazine.

1963: The Playboy Forum debuts for *Playboy* readers to debate issues related to the Playboy Philosophy. Hugh Hefner is arrested on charges of obscenity.

1964: Playboy Theater opens in Chicago.

1965: The Playboy Foundation is founded. Hugh Hefner purchases the new 37-story Playboy headquarters building in Chicago. The first African American Playmate appears in the March issue of *Playboy*.

1966: New Playboy headquarters opens in Chicago and is named the Playboy Building. London Playboy Club and Casino opens.

1967: Hugh Hefner appears on the cover of *Time* magazine for a story called, "The Pursuit of Hedonism", catapulting his position as a celebrity and influencer to new heights.

A BRAND RISES DESPITE THE NAYSAYERS—THE 1960s

1968: The Playboy Mansion in Chicago becomes the sight of numerous events for the Democratic Party. Playboy Resort opens in Geneva, Wisconsin. *Playboy After Dark* premiers on CBS and is syndicated nationally. *Playboy* magazine circulation surpasses 5.5 million copies per month.

1969: Hugh Hefner purchases the Playboy jet and names it Big Bunny. The *London Sunday Times* selects Hugh Hefner as one of the most influential people of the century. Playboy company annual sales reach $96 million.

CHAPTER 5

GROWTH EXPLOSION

I never started the company because I wanted to be hugely successful as a company. For me, this has always been from the heart. It had very little to do with money.

Hugh Hefner, 1999 Interview
with *The New Yorker*

If the 1950s are to be considered successful for Playboy, then the 1960s would have to be called unimaginable. At the start of a new decade, circulation of *Playboy* magazine was enjoying a comfortable 1 million copies per month with revenues of over $5 million pouring in each year. Playboy had made its mark and was here to stay. By 1961, the company grew to become a $20 million empire, and by 1969, yearly sales hit $96 million with circulation exceeding 5.5 million per month. Timing again played an important role in the growth of the Playboy brand when the 1960s ushered in a broader call for a sexual revolution that swept across America. Playboy stood proudly in the forefront of the call for change, and Hugh Hefner spoke out vehemently for the freedoms he felt all people should enjoy. Publicity and the buzz around Hugh Hefner and Playboy continued to grow, and ongoing brand extensions in the 1960s expanded the brand's reach significantly.

The first months of the 1960s brought the *Playboy's Penthouse* television program into homes around the country, which further solidified Playboy as both an experience and relationship brand as discussed in Chapter 4. At the same time, the first Playboy Club opened its doors in Chicago on February 29, 1960. The private Playboy Club would provide a new way for consumers to experience the brand and live the lifestyle the brand promised. In simplest terms, it brought the Playboy brand to life.

The Chicago Playboy Club was elaborate in design with an exclusive style to match the lifestyle depicted in the pages of *Playboy* magazine. The 5-story club was laid out to emulate a bachelor's fantasy apartment with dining, living, and entertainment areas. At the heart of the club were the Playboy bunnies that served drinks and acted as hosts. Bunnies were expected to abide by a very strict code of appearance and behavior, outlined in great detail by Keith Hefner in the *Playboy Club Bunny Manual*. The entire Playboy Club experience from the ambiance to the bunnies and everything in between had to effectively portray the Playboy brand image and brand promise to ensure the experience consumers had once they entered through the club's doors was consistent with the fantasy depicted in the pages of *Playboy* magazine and befitting of Hugh Hefner, himself.

To become a Playboy Club member and gain entry into the fantasy, a $50 one-time fee was required. Once that fee was paid, members were given a Playboy key emblazoned with the Playboy bunny logo on it, and they could enter the club at anytime for the rest of their lives. Being a member of the Playboy Club held a mystique that consumers wore like a badge of honor. It tied in perfectly with the relationship brand, and within the first year, over 50,000 people had paid their $50 each to become members. Over the next several years, 15 more Playboy Clubs would open around the United States in cities such as Miami, New Orleans, Phoenix, New York, Los Angeles, San Francisco, Detroit, Baltimore, Boston, Atlanta, and Kansas City with membership quickly growing to 500,000 and eventually to 1 million. In 1966, Playboy made its first move to expand outside the United States when a new Playboy Club and Casino opened in London, England, opening the doors to growth even wider than they had been before. The London gaming business would quickly grow to be very lucrative for the Playboy company and would open more opportunities for Hugh Hefner to pursue additional brand extensions.

The success of Playboy and the image the brand portrayed was legendary, and the entertainment world took notice. As Playboy grew, more and more popular writers were submitting articles for publication in the pages of *Playboy* magazine. In September 1962, the Playboy Interview debuted, and quickly celebrities from entertainment, sports, music, politics, and more were lining up to be featured. Through the award-winning articles and in-depth Playboy Interviews, consumers found new ways to connect with the Playboy brand. In less than a decade, Playboy had gone from an $8,000 risk to a multimillion-dollar media empire that was getting noticed around the world.

Ironically, Hugh Hefner was becoming more reclusive at the same time that the Playboy brand was reaching new heights of popularity (and criticism). *Playboy's Penthouse* ended after a 2-year run, and the brand champion was lost in the political and cultural struggles of the 1960s. As a result, he became increasingly absent from the public eye. Parties continued at the Playboy Mansion, but Hefner would make casual appearances then disappear to his bedroom to work. He became completely absorbed in recreating *Playboy* as not just a men's lifestyle magazine, but also a publication that addressed the social, political, and cultural inequalities of the time.

Despite Hefner's visible absence in the 1960s, the brand continued to grow and expand. As luck would have it, his absence simply fueled the mystique that surrounded him and made people more interested in the man behind the Playboy brand. Brand extensions in the 1960s included Playboy Tours offering vacation packages, and merchandise with the Playboy bunny logo continued to extend into new categories such as golf equipment, lighters, calendars, and more.

The Playboy Theater opened in Chicago on September 28, 1964, providing yet another way for consumers to experience the high-culture lifestyle depicted within *Playboy* magazine. A record label, television and movie company, and more were added to the Playboy roster during the same decade. In addition, Playboy-related books continued to be released, including *The Playboy Gourmet*, which provided information about food, drinks, and entertainment, *The Bedside Playboy*, featuring a compilation of the best articles and stories taken from the pages of *Playboy* magazine, and *LeRoy Neiman Portfolio* and *Alberto Vargas Portfolio*, collections of the artists' drawings that were originally published in *Playboy* magazine. In short, there was something for every Playboy consumer to enjoy and further experience the brand.

Of course, Hefner and Playboy did not survive the 1960s without some failures. An entertainment magazine, *Show Business Illustrated*, failed, and a movie about Hefner's life fell apart before a script could be agreed upon. However, most of the *Playboy* world turned to gold in the 1960s.

Hugh Hefner may have been a recluse in the first half of the 1960s, but he still maintained tight control over the Playboy brand. All brand extensions, pieces of merchandise, books, projects, interviews, and so on had to be approved by Hefner. His tight grip on the Playboy brand continued to ensure that a level of consistency was maintained with

A BRAND RISES DESPITE THE NAYSAYERS—THE 1960s

> **BOX 5.1** The Hard Rock Cafe and Jack Daniels as experience brands
>
> The Hard Rock Cafe is another example of a brand that creates experiences through brand extensions that not only surround consumers but also allow them to become emotionally involved with the brand. Through Hard Rock branded restaurants, stores, merchandise, hotels, casinos, nightclubs, and more, the company provides experiences and allows consumers to pick and choose the ways they want to connect with the brand. The varied experiences appeal to a wide audience but are varied enough that they appeal to specific subsegments of the broader audience. By creating different branded extensions and experiences, new consumers can be introduced to the brand and are likely to take the initiative to experience the brand in additional ways if that first introduction meets their expectations.
>
> Jack Daniels also effectively uses brand extensions to create complete brand experiences. While Jack Daniels is first and foremost a brand of whiskey, extensions have allowed consumers to experience the brand in a variety of ways through merchandise like clothing, bar accessories, home decor, games, and fashion accessories. The Jack Daniels brand can also be found in the cooking aisles at supermarkets through branded seasonings, rubs, and ingredients as well as on restaurant dining menus. For example, the TGI Fridays restaurant chain carries a full line of Jack Daniels branded menu items, including steak dishes, shrimp dishes, and more.

all brand extensions and branded experiences (see Box 5.1 for more examples of brand extensions that create brand experiences). The goal was still to present a full entertainment package that provided consumers with the tools they needed to experience the brand in their own ways, live the brand promise, and attain the fantasy life depicted in *Playboy* magazine. To that end, Hefner may not have been the best businessman, but he was a fierce brand guardian.

A BRAND GROWS TOO BIG

By the late 1960s, brand extensions reached a frenzied pace. A Playboy Resort opened in Lake Geneva, Wisconsin, and later in Great Gorge,

New Jersey. The resorts included restaurants, bars, shopping, entertainment, sports, recreation, and more targeted to affluent consumers. A Playboy Limousine company was also created. The brand began to lose focus but succeeded based on the strong relationships it had developed with consumers and the momentum it carried with it. The writing was on the wall, however, that the momentum could not be sustained with assets spread in so many directions, many of which Playboy's leaders had little experience with or expertise in. Clearly, the brand extensions of the 1960s represented a somewhat misguided growth strategy (see Box 5.2 for more information about brand extension strategies and risks). However, the laws of contraction and focus tell marketers that a brand is stronger with a tighter focus than a diluted, over-extended brand is as follows.

Brand Focus

Brand focus can be directly related to brand positioning. What *space* does your brand *occupy* in consumer's minds and in the marketplace? Taking the law of brand positioning a step further, one can ask, what *word* does your brand *own* in consumer's minds? That is brand focus—the single word (or phrase) your brand owns in the minds of consumers. For the Playboy brand, the word started out as "sex." Although Hugh Hefner never believed his magazine was about sex alone and frequently cited the fact that no more than 5% of any issue of *Playboy* magazine contained photographs of nude or semi-nude women in the early days, consumers nevertheless associated the brand with sex. It gave the brand power and a singular focus that enabled it to grow quickly.

BOX 5.2 Brand extension strategies and risks

Companies typically extend brands for several primary reasons:

1. *To ease the costs associated with launching a new product.* Since an established brand is already known, a company can bypass much of the marketing costs related to developing brand awareness and recognition. Automobile manufacturers like Toyota use this brand

extension strategy frequently when they add new car models to an existing product line under the same brand name (e.g., the Toyota Aveo, Toyota Camry, Toyota Corolla, Toyota Matrix, and so on).

2. *To reduce the risk associated with launching a new product.* In simplest terms, an established brand name brings with it preconceived perceptions for that brand, even when introduced to a new category, and that brand name can establish instant acceptance. For example, when Apple entered the mobile phone market, the brand was welcomed because it was already trusted and consumers had established expectations for it, regardless of the market it entered.

3. *To extend a brand's lifecycle by offering new ways for consumers to experience it.* As consumer preferences and the marketplace evolve, a company often has to launch new products and services to meet those needs and demands. For example, companies like Coca-Cola launch various ways for consumers to drink their products by offering them in new package sizes, new flavors, and so on to meet changing consumer needs and demands.

4. *To spread dependence on a single product or product line.* It's never a good idea for a company to put all of its eggs in one basket. In order to spread dependency and associated risk, companies can extend an existing brand. If one product under the brand umbrella fails, the investments already made in brand building do not necessarily have to fail, too. Examples include Disney Wine, Life Savers Soda, and Colgate Kitchen Entrees. Each of these brand extensions were quick failures, but the parent brand was strong enough to survive.

The problem for Playboy in the 1960s was following a strategy of extending the brand to meet Hugh Hefner's personal whims and interests rather than analyzing extension opportunities and selecting only those that truly fit the brand and the company. Not all brand extensions succeed, which is something Hugh Hefner and Playboy wouldn't learn until the 1970s. There are inherent risks in extending a brand such as:

- Diluting the strength of the brand by over-saturating the market with it.
- Confusing consumers by extending the brand into markets, products, or services that run counter to the brand's original promise.

- Weakening the brand's overall equity by spreading it too thin with far-reaching links back to the parent brand.
- Hurting the parent brand if extensions fail or drive negative publicity.
- Weakening the brand's performances because resources are spread too thin to sustain them.
- Damaging the parent brand because the expertise is not available in the varied categories where the brand has expanded in order to make them all thrive.
- While brand extensions are tempting, they should not be implemented without careful analysis from both ends of the spectrum—both the opportunity for the brand extension to succeed *and* the potential effects on the parent brand. This is the step that Playboy often skipped as the rewards from short-term growth frequently outweighed long-term strategic planning.

In the 1960s, as Hugh Hefner's vision of Playboy expanded to include a social and political agenda, consumers inevitably became confused. The brand they so closely associated with sex now encompassed much more. Consumers had to choose whether they could get on board with the broader brand strategy or not. As luck would have it, the vast majority of *Playboy* readers either held similar political and social views and welcomed the broader brand strategy, or they completely ignored it and decidedly paid attention only to the original brand focus as well as the available Playboy experiences that personally appealed to them which they could not easily find elsewhere. Either way, the brand continued to thrive during the 1960s despite a brand strategy that could have led to massive confusion and consumer rejection.

Brand Contraction

Brand contraction relates directly to brand focus. The accepted argument is this—brands are stronger when their focus is narrowed (see Box 5.3 for examples of brands that have been forced to contract). As the 1960s progressed, the Playboy brand extended into multiple markets and became a true entertainment, media, and real estate empire. Focus was lost, and the brand could have suffered immediately and

A BRAND RISES DESPITE THE NAYSAYERS—THE 1960s

BOX 5.3 Examples of brands forced to contract

Playboy is not the only brand that has lost focus at some point during its lifecycle and been forced to contract. For example, AT&T grew in the 1990s to be one of the largest and broadest reaching companies in the world with irons in a wide variety of fires. It started out with a primary brand focus on telecommunications delivery. In the United States, AT&T was known as the phone company. However, by the mid-1990s, the company extended its brand to include telecommunications equipment manufacturing (large and small), retail stores, computers, automated teller machines (ATMs), equipment leasing, equipment reselling, auto financing, credit cards, and more.

In 1996, the company could no longer sustain its broad brand extensions and was forced to break up into three separate companies. The AT&T name continued to be used for the telephone service business while the equipment manufacturing division took the Lucent Technologies name, and the computer-related business reverted to its original NCR brand name. Today, the three companies continue to operate separate and distinctively unrelated businesses.

Another example of a brand that lost focus and found itself in the position where brand contraction was required is IBM which began its rise by focusing on developing mainframe computers. As the market and the world changed, IBM was slow to change with it. Other companies jumped in and became market leaders in categories such as personal computers. IBM attempted to compete but eventually the company became a victim of its own brand extensions. With hands in personal computers, printing, copiers, telephones, and a myriad of other products, IBM had lost brand focus, and over the course of many years, slowly contracted by selling businesses that did not complement the company's core competencies and slowly redefining its business and brand to meet the needs of the new marketplace. IBM continues to struggle in a highly competitive industry. Like Playboy, IBM is the victim of its own success and is often too reactionary to regain a position as market leader.

immensely. However, Hugh Hefner and Playboy were in the right place at the right time and again, momentum was on their side.

Consumers wanted and *needed* a vehicle like Playboy to voice the liberal opinions of a growing minority. Playboy became a symbol of the sexual revolution, the pursuit of personal freedom, and the fight for equality that so many people in the United States desired in the 1960s. Despite a focus that was arguably too broad and a brand extension strategy that most marketing experts would raise a red flag at, Playboy continued to prosper in the 1960s, simply because it spoke to a growing niche audience and filled a gap. In other words, it continued to fulfill the fundamental business truth—it's easier to create a product to fulfill an existing need than it is to create a perceived need to fulfill the business objectives of an existing product.

However, as Hugh Hefner became more entrenched in the politics of the decade (as discussed in Chapter 6) than the business side of his company, focus was hard to find. A magazine that once promoted itself as a men's lifestyle publication was shifting to a political rag with a highly liberal lean to the left. Had the momentum not been so strong and the social call for sexual and personal freedom and equality not been so loud in the 1960s, Playboy may have suffered. Instead, the brand and company were able to ride the wave of a cry for change throughout the 1960s and well into the 1970s before an inevitable shift in momentum occurred. But the law of brand contraction would eventually come to haunt Hefner and Playboy.

The question for Playboy in the 1960s was how long the good times could last? How long could a single company support a broad and unfocused brand strategy? As the decade wore on, the end was nowhere in sight. Sales continued to grow and profits kept rolling in. Hugh Hefner was a multimillionaire, and the Playboy brand was set to expand to become a global icon.

In 1968, a new Playboy-branded television show hosted by Hugh Hefner, *Playboy After Dark*, premiered on CBS and was syndicated nationally. The lifestyle depicted in the early days of Playboy and even in the first Playboy branded television program, *Playboy's Penthouse*, was no longer singularly focused on self-fulfillment. Now, the brand held social, political, religious, and cultural connotations, and *Playboy After Dark* took on new meaning (see Chapter 7 for more information about *Playboy After Dark*). The Playboy party continued, but the Playboy fantasy had evolved and would never be quite the same again. Soon Hugh Hefner and Playboy would face attacks from all sides of the political, religious, and social debates of the time, including attacks from its core audience. The world had changed and Playboy had changed with it, but the world may not have wanted Playboy to change with it after all. It seemed sex, drugs, and rock and roll make good bed fellows, but sex, drugs, and politics did not—at least not for long.

CHAPTER 6

DEFENDING THE BRAND

I never thought of Playboy as a sex magazine. It was a lifestyle magazine.

Hugh Hefner, 2003 Interview
with Charlie Rose

American society changed dramatically in the 1960s. The inward-looking, family-centric norms of social behavior were no longer enough for people as communication traveled faster, and they found themselves with more leisure time thanks to better technology. People began to speak out against social inequalities and governmental leadership they didn't agree with. The simple, self-indulgent lifestyle depicted on the pages of *Playboy* had to change with society in order to remain relevant. For Hugh Hefner, the goal wasn't so much to retain brand relevancy as it was to be seen as a thought leader defending personal freedoms and fighting against the inequalities he detested for so long.

Secure in his magazine's position and buoyed by his impression of his influence upon American society, Hugh Hefner made a bold decision to expand the content of *Playboy* in the 1960s. Despite setting clear expectations for the brand in the introduction of the first issue in December 1953, which stated, "Affairs of the state will be out of our province," Hefner saw it as his duty in his ongoing pursuit for personal freedoms to add a social, cultural, and political bend to the magazine. The men's lifestyle magazine became an agent of change for the world of politics and society, questioning the very norms and rules that Hefner found so repressive during his youth and even more hypocritical as an adult.

A BRAND RISES DESPITE THE NAYSAYERS—THE 1960s

In the early 1960s, Hefner consciously turned *Playboy* magazine in a new direction. He wanted *Playboy* to not just be a *part* of the change that was happening around him but to *lead* that change. *Playboy* magazine would still include the features and pictorials consumers expected from the men's lifestyle brand. For example, the *Playboy* Advisor debuted in 1960, which included Hefner's complete set of instructions to create answers to common questions about dating, fashion, dining, entertaining, and so on. The feature continues to run half a century later. However, Hugh Hefner believed that for *Playboy* to continue to grow, the focus had to shift to the issues of the time that were standing in the way of readers living the fantasy life depicted in *Playboy* magazine. In a move that could have isolated core consumers, Hefner added commentaries to the pages of *Playboy* on subjects related to society, culture, religion, and politics. As luck would have it, his decision paid off, and *Playboy* became a symbol of the liberal voice of the young Baby Boomer generation in the 1960s (see Box 6.1 for more information on the Baby Boomer generation).

BOX 6.1 The Baby Boomer Generation

Members of the Baby Boomer Generation were born between approximately 1946 and 1954 and became a force to be reckoned with when they reached adulthood simply because of their vast numbers (there are over 76 million members of the Baby Boomer Generation compared to 50 million members of the Silent Generation before it). The Baby Boomer Generation is characterized as the first generation that grew up with an expectation that the world and their lives would be better than the generation before it. The generation enjoyed relative privilege and prosperity, being called the healthiest and wealthiest generation (up to that time).

Members of the Baby Boomer generation grew up with a sense of entitlement and fought against social inequities in an effort to change reserved and repressive political, religious, and social norms. Events such as the civil rights movement, the birth of the feminist movement, anti-war protests, sit-ins, and more would be the legacy of a generation focused on individual rights, social causes, freedom, and equality. Baby Boomers were optimistic and truly believed they could force the changes they fought for into action.

THE PLAYBOY PHILOSOPHY

While the American people may have been the catalyst for change in the 1960s, Playboy stood as a tangible symbol of the change many people were not yet ready to embrace. Therefore, Playboy and Hugh Hefner became targets of attacks from a long list of people and groups. Both Hugh Hefner and Playboy were getting massive amounts of publicity from the press. Articles in magazine such as *Time*, *The Wall Street Journal*, *The New Yorker*, and more acknowledged the business successes of Hefner and Playboy but not without admonishing the man and the brand for representing the changes conservative Americans were not yet ready for. Hefner appeared in television documentaries and interviews on major programs, including *Firing Line* with Warren Buffet, *The Today Show* on NBC, and *The Jack Paar Show* to defend himself, his brand, and his views.

Hefner and Playboy became inseparable in people's minds and brought both the man and the brand to new audiences. Hugh Hefner positioned himself and his magazine as purveyors of sexual liberty, civil rights, and civil liberties with a focus on freedom of speech and equality. Not everyone agreed with him though, and that controversy drove the buzz about Hefner and Playboy even louder than it was in the 1950s. As a result, interest in Hefner and his brand spread far and wide, and the business of Playboy continued to grow and thrive.

As early as 1960, Hefner took steps to move *Playboy* magazine in a more political direction when he started the Playboy Panel and invited readers to debate issues of the day. By inviting consumers to become personally involved through the Playboy Panel, Hefner was creating a deeper emotional connection to the Playboy brand that a specific segment of consumers responded to. The Playboy Panel allowed consumers to choose a new way to experience the inclusive Playboy brand, and it invited consumers to take control of that experience.

The Playboy Panel could be compared to the online social media marketing of the 21st century where user generated content and brand interactivity reigns supreme. Anytime consumers are allowed to control their personal interaction with a brand, a deeper connection with the brand develops. As such, Playboy had another opportunity to become a stronger relationship brand through the Playboy Panel. Hugh Hefner certainly didn't realize what he was doing at the time in terms of taking steps to build a strong relationship brand, but fortunately, that is exactly what happened. Consumers got involved and Playboy and Hugh Hefner's stars continued to rise.

A BRAND RISES DESPITE THE NAYSAYERS—THE 1960s

In the early 1960s, Hefner nearly disappeared from the public eye, and over the course of several years, espoused what he referred to as the *Playboy* editorial credo mixed with his own observations of society and the role of *Playboy* within it. What resulted was a vociferous response from people of all walks of life. Hefner obsessed over what he called "The Playboy Philosophy," and ultimately published 25 installments over the course of a 3-year period, including 150,000 words dedicated to his opinions about society, culture, politics, and the world in the 1960s. Hefner emerged from his bedroom long enough to attend interviews to defend his Playboy Philosophy. He started the Playboy Forum in 1963, so *Playboy* readers could voice their opinions about the Playboy Philosophy, and he even conducted a college-speaking tour in 1965 to discuss his philosophy with a core target audience.

From the early to mid-1960s, the Playboy Philosophy was all-consuming for Hugh Hefner. While it may have alienated some original *Playboy* consumers who would undoubtedly be confused by the brand shift, a greater number of people were intrigued, either because they agreed with him or they were caught up in the publicity buzz surrounding Hefner and *Playboy*. The result brought continued growth to *Playboy*, which allowed the brand to extend to more markets and categories than ever before, as discussed in Chapter 5. It also brought Hefner notoriety and made him a figurehead for civil liberty. In 1962, he received one of his earliest awards for his commitment to the fight for equality.

When Hefner was arrested in 1963 and eventually acquitted on charges of obscenity due to nude pictures of Jayne Mansfield that appeared in *Playboy* magazine, he emerged as a symbol of the defense of free speech. In short, he symbolized the freedom that a growing group of Americans wanted, and he wasn't afraid to speak out about it as a leading face of the movement. The world took notice, and in 1969, the *London Sunday Times* selected Hugh Hefner as one of the most influential people of the century.

PLAYBOY AS AN INCLUSIVE BRAND

Playboy is not just a relationship brand for individuals, but rather, it is a relationship brand for everyone. In other words, from the beginning, it was a brand accessible to people from all ethnicities, backgrounds, religions, and so on. From the early days of his youth, Hugh Hefner detested prejudice and inequality, so it's not surprising that the brand he created was open to anyone to enjoy. In many ways, Hugh Hefner and Playboy were the ultimate symbols of racial equality in the 1960s.

During a time when it was unheard of for people from mixed cultures to appear in a social setting together, *Playboy's Penthouse* and *Playboy After Dark* always included a diverse cast of entertainers and partygoers. The doors of the Playboy Clubs were open to performers and guests of all races and religions. In fact, when the Playboy Club in New Orleans was sold to a franchisor in the 1960s and Hefner heard that the franchise was not admitting African American patrons to the club, he repurchased it to ensure that the doors were open to all guests who wanted to enjoy the Playboy lifestyle. In other words, there were no boundaries to who could experience the Playboy fantasy.

The first African American Playmate appeared in *Playboy* magazine in March 1965, a time when racial segregation was still common in many parts of the country. *Playboy* broke down walls and paved a path for societal, cultural, and political changes and then followed through on its newly formed brand promise by continually speaking out against inequality and denial of freedoms. However, with Hugh Hefner and Playboy always comes controversy, and even Hefner's attempts to fight for civil liberties would be challenged.

By the latter half of the 1960s, many of the liberties Hefner spoke so vocally about in the pages of *Playboy* magazine were coming to fruition. However, a new movement, led by a group of women called feminists, would challenge Hefner and the Playboy brand in a new way. For many years, Hefner positioned *Playboy* as a men's lifestyle magazine, stating in interviews that women shouldn't be equal to men but rather complementary to men. It was the accepted point of view in the 1950s and had yet to be questioned or challenged. Eventually, those words would come back to haunt Hefner. He would be labeled as a hypocrite who fought for equality, but not for *all* people. In 1963, now famous journalist Gloria Steinem went undercover as a Playboy Club Bunny, and Hefner's cover was blown. She wrote a scathing exposé outlining exactly how Playboy repressed women and positioned Hefner and Playboy as symbols of the anti-feminist movement (see Box 6.2 for more information about Steinem's "I Was a Playboy Bunny").

The battle between feminists and Playboy would evolve in the 1970s, but the writing was on the wall as early as 1963 that challenges were looming ahead, and a new long-term brand strategy was desperately needed. In the 1960s, Playboy focused on short-term growth, taking a lesson from the pages of its own magazine and enjoying

A BRAND RISES DESPITE THE NAYSAYERS—THE 1960s

> **BOX 6.2** "I Was a Playboy Bunny" by Gloria Steinem
>
> In 1963, a young journalist named Gloria Steinem was trying to get her career started. She accepted an assignment from *Show* magazine to go undercover at the New York City Playboy Club as a Playboy Bunny in order to learn what went on behind the scenes, and hopefully, expose the brand as degrading, repressive, and unfair to female workers. Steinem began her assignment thinking she'd go on a few interviews and develop opinions from that, but in a short amount of time she found herself hired and donning a blue bunny costume. She completed the necessary Playboy Bunny training and worked at the New York City Playboy Club for approximately 1 month.
>
> From that experience, Steinem drew a number of conclusions about Playboy, most of them very negative and highly damaging to the Playboy brand. She claimed that Playboy offered applicants $200–$300 per week, but once they started working, they learned that they would only make $12 per day until they were promoted to the more lucrative position of Table Bunny. At a time when the Feminist Movement was beginning to pick up steam, Steinem's article focused on the long Playboy Bunny work hours claiming women were grossly underpaid and continually degraded by male employees and customers. Many Playboy Bunnies disagreed with Steinem's depiction of their lives, but in a world where women's issues were growing stronger everyday, the story resonated with a wide audience. When *Esquire* published the article, the story exploded, and so did both Steinem's career and her position as a feminist.
>
> For Playboy, the article was just one more piece of negative publicity that Hugh Hefner had to fight, and fight it he did. At the time, Hugh Hefner truly did not believe that he was exploiting women in *Playboy* magazine. He actually believed in the 1960s that he was liberating women. Unfortunately, for Hugh Hefner and the Playboy empire, Steinem's article would be the go-to piece for people looking for evidence against the Playboy brand for many years to come.

short-term, self-satisfying gains with little regard to long-term sustainability. However, with much of the country calling for change in the 1960s, Playboy became a symbol of certain aspects of that change and continued to thrive. Was it dumb luck or Hugh Hefner's genius that helped Playboy thrive in the 1960s? Again, it seems like a case

BOX 6.3 How Toyota and Pepsi leveraged the macro environment with different results

In the 2000s, consumers were more concerned about the environment and the rising price of gasoline than ever before. Toyota recognized that growing concern and took steps to make the changing macro environment benefit the brand and the company by developing a more environmentally-friendly vehicle, the Prius. It took a few years for the Prius to become popular, but when gas prices soared in 2008, the number of consumers in the United States who traded in their gas-guzzling SUVs for smaller cars and environmentally-friendly cars such as the Toyota Prius skyrocketed. Toyota used a proactive strategy to predict future car-buying behaviors based on the macro environment, and doing so allowed the company to experience smaller losses during the economic downturn of the late 2000s than most other automobile manufacturers around the world.

Another example of leveraging the macro environment to extend a brand comes from Pepsi-Cola. In the early 1990s, the environment and healthy living became the causes du jour. Consumers from all parts of the world became more concerned about both causes, and consumer-product companies reacted to that raised social awareness by redefining their brands as environmentally friendly and health-conscious. One of the simplest and earliest changes that companies made in the early 1990s was changing consumer product manufacturing processes to make existing products appear more environmentally friendly and thus, healthier, too. For example, Ivory soap which was always known (and advertised) as having a creamy white substance, infused with milk, suddenly became a clear liquid and "clean." The "clear" fad raced across various categories and markets. For many, it worked, but for some, it was a brand extension that didn't enhance the brand and in fact, confused consumers. Crystal Pepsi was one of those products. Consumers simply did not believe the "clear" Pepsi message. In fact, even *Saturday Night Live* cast members questioned the common sense for Crystal Pepsi with its own parody commercial for Crystal Gravy. Within a year, Pepsi pulled Crystal Pepsi from its product line amid low sales volumes.

of being in the right place at the right time coupled with filling a gap that no one else was willing to take a risk on.

In the 1960s, as it did a decade earlier, the macro environment played a significant role in the growth and success of the Playboy brand (see Box 6.3 for examples of brands that leveraged the macro environment), and as in the 1950s, consumers felt a strong emotional involvement to the Playboy brand. However, in the 1960s, that emotional involvement took on a new level of importance as the brand came to symbolize a cultural movement that affected an audience much larger than the core Playboy consumer market. It could be argued that without the macro environmental factors of the 1960s, *Playboy* would have grown to be a popular men's magazine similar to others in the market, but once it took on a political agenda, the audience potential grew significantly. In the 1960s, Playboy grew to become a strong cult brand (see Chapter 7 for more information about Playboy as a cult brand) and developed a loyal following unknown previously within the magazine publishing industry.

Playboy in the 1960s became even stronger as an emotional brand. Not only did the brand hit upon emotional triggers such as self-gratification and pleasure, but it also hit upon triggers no one expected in the early days. Certainly, when *Playboy* debuted in 1953, no one could have imagined that less than two decades later the magazine would include "Playboy's Political Preference Chart" which graded candidates running for election in 1970 based on their liberal views. Alternately, who would have thought when the Chicago Playboy Mansion opened in 1959, a symbol of self-gratification and pleasure, that just 15 years later, it would be the site of numerous events for the Democratic Party? Again, one could argue that the changes to the Playboy brand were genius in terms of growing the brand quickly or crazy in terms of extending the brand too far beyond its niche and focus to the point where it couldn't be sustained over the long run. Whichever school of thought you align with, however, one thing is for certain, it worked, at least for awhile.

CHAPTER 7

LIVING THE BRAND

That's part of it, and it's not entirely accidental.
Hugh Hefner discussing the fact that part of Playboy's success comes from the publicity about his own life in a 2003 interview with Greg Jackson of ABC News

While spending a great deal of time defending the Playboy brand in the 1960s, Hugh Hefner's role as the face of the Playboy brand also grew. He seized opportunities to defend the Playboy Philosophy in magazines and newspapers and on television. A Canadian documentary about Hefner called *The Most* premiered in 1961, and Hefner appeared on television shows as diverse as Warren Buffet's *Firing Line* to *The Tonight* Show and *Laugh-In*. Articles and interviews with Hefner appeared in magazines and newspapers as varied as *BusinessWeek*, *Barron's*, *Newsweek*, and *Mad* magazine. Hefner and Playboy were everywhere, and as Hefner's star rose, so did Playboy's earnings. In the 1960s, Hefner became the very thing that enamored him most during his youth—a celebrity.

The early 1960s also brought Hugh Hefner and Playboy to a global audience. While global brand growth wouldn't be a focus until a decade later, the start of the 1960s introduced Hugh Hefner and Playboy to people in Italy, Germany, England, South America, and more as magazines around the world published articles about the man and his brand. The increased exposure allowed Playboy to expand its reach through numerous brand extensions, including an extravagant Playboy Club and Casino in London, England, which opened in 1966 and expanded quickly to a large number of locations in the United Kingdom offering a variety of gaming options such as off-track betting and bingo in addition to more traditional casinos.

While Hefner spent much of the 1960s defending *Playboy*, well-known writers were contributing articles and bigger celebrities were participating in Playboy Interviews (see Box 7.1 for more information about celebrities and acclaimed authors in Playboy during the 1960s). To ensure the content of *Playboy* was always of the best quality and consistent with the Playboy brand image, the company made a conscious decision to pay writers more for submissions than any other magazine.

The 1960s also brought opportunities for Playboy to expand into corporate giving. In 1965, the Playboy Foundation was created to bring the Playboy Philosophy to life. The organization provides grants and donations to organizations dedicated to fighting censorship,

---

BOX 7.1 Celebrities and writers in Playboy during the 1960s

During the 1960s, *Playboy* magazine met Hugh Hefner's goals of being a high quality literary magazine. Acclaimed writers contributed compelling content, including

- Ray Bradbury
- Roald Dahl
- Ian Fleming (the character of James Bond debuted on the pages of *Playboy*)
- Alex Haley
- Ernest Hemingway
- John Irving
- James Jones
- Jack Kerouac
- Carl Sandburg
- Irwin Shaw
- John Steinbeck
- John Updike
- Kurt Vonnegut Jr. and more

Playboy magazine also attracted big name celebrities from Hollywood, politics, sports, and social movements for Playboy Interviews, including

- Miles Davis
- Peter Sellers
- Jackie Gleason
- Frank Sinatra
- Helen Gurley Brown
- Malcolm X
- Richard Burton
- Jimmy Hoffa
- Albert Schweitzer
- Vladimir Nabokov
- Jack Lemmon
- Ingmar Bergman
- Salvador Dali
- Cassius Clay (Muhammad Ali)
- Martin Luther King Jr.
- The Beatles
- Jean-Paul Sartre
- Peter O'Toole
- Sean Connery
- Princess Grace
- Bob Dylan
- Mel Brooks
- Sammy Davis Jr.
- Fidel Castro
- Orson Welles
- Woody Allen
- Johnny Carson
- Norman Mailer
- Truman Capote

A BRAND RISES DESPITE THE NAYSAYERS—THE 1960s

- Paul Newman
- Stanley Kubrick
- Ralph Nader
- Bill Cosby
- Gore Vidal
- Jesse Jackson
- Joe Namath and more.

advocating the First Amendment, and fighting for sexual freedoms. The foundation also represented a direct response to the people who attacked Hefner and the Playboy brand in the 1960s by turning negative publicity into a positive for the company.

Interestingly, as the focus of Playboy shifted to take on the liberal political voice of its founder, the face of the brand became less visible. During the early years of the 1960s, when Hugh Hefner focused completely on The Playboy Philosophy and its defense, the brand lost some sight of its core value proposition—living the good life people deserve. It seemed priorities changed and fighting to ensure more people could attain personal freedoms took precedence over actually living the good life. Hefner's reclusive, workaholic mannerisms of the early to mid-1960s supported the brand shift as did the content in the pages of *Playboy* magazine. However, consumers were already so emotionally involved in the original incarnation of the Playboy brand that the brand promise continued to thrive in Playboy Clubs, Playboy Resorts, and so on. In other words, consumers continued to experience the brand and personalize it in their own ways regardless of Hugh Hefner's repositioning of the magazine.

HUGH HEFNER REINVENTS HIMSELF FOR THE THIRD TIME

As the 1960s wore on, Hugh Hefner reinvented himself again. The brand champion emerged from the depths of the Chicago Playboy Mansion and put aside his Playboy Philosophy to re-enter the world as the symbol of the Playboy lifestyle. However, that lifestyle now included an essential regard for the politics and social inequalities of the time.

LIVING THE BRAND

In 1967, Hugh Hefner decided to reinvent himself as the celebrity he now believed himself to be. Not only did he change himself outwardly with a new wardrobe and so on, but he also extricated himself from much of the daily workings of the Playboy company he had previously controlled in every way. He delegated responsibilities and presented himself to the public as an influential public figure. His transformation ushered in a new buzz about the Playboy brand as parties at the Playboy Mansion grew in terms of frequency and size as well as in terms of the lurid stories they conjured.

To go along with the bigger-than-ever mentality of Hugh Hefner and the Playboy brand of the late 1960s, a new Playboy headquarters building opened in Chicago in 1966. The 37-story skyscraper was big and bold with gigantic lighted letters spelling out "Playboy Building" across the roof, reminiscent of the Hollywood sign in the hills of Los Angeles, California. The Playboy brand was the ultimate symbol of excess again, and that brand message was communicated even more clearly when Hefner purchased his own DC-9 jet in 1969, painted it black, and put the Playboy bunny logo on it. He called it Big Bunny, hired a crew of eight "Jet Bunnies," and hosted parties in the sky. The jet included a bedroom, movie room, game room, dining room, and more and became a flying Playboy Club. At a time when very few people owned their own jets, Big Bunny represented the ultimate symbol of a man living the brand promise.

Brand extensions in the late 1960s took their cue from the excessive lifestyle that came to be Hugh Hefner's and the new Playboy fantasy. For example, the Playboy Resorts in Wisconsin and New Jersey included all the bells and whistles one would expect from the now lavish Playboy lifestyle. Shopping, dining, entertainment, skiing, stage shows, game rooms, tennis courts, golf courses, and bars catered to affluent guests who wanted to experience the Playboy brand. Furthermore, the second *Playboy* television show, *Playboy After Dark*, debuted in 1968 and further demonstrated the allure of the excessive Playboy lifestyle. Unlike the original *Playboy's Penthouse*, the new Playboy television show was Hollywood grown. In other words, it was filmed in full-color with all the Hollywood accoutrements one would expect from a brand that advocated extravagant living like Playboy. Guests were big, performances were big, and the party was bigger. This was the Playboy brand of the late 1960s. It had grown up and evolved, but at the heart of the brand was still the desire for personal freedom and satisfaction above all else. No one symbolized that fantasy better than Hugh Hefner, the ultimate brand champion.

> **BOX 7.2** The inclusive brand strategy of Barack Obama's 2008 U.S. Presidential Campaign
>
> In 2008, U.S. Senator Barack Obama set out to become the 44th president of the United States. He was young, he was inexperienced, and he was African American. All three points could work against him, but instead, they helped him. In response to the exclusive marketing strategy employed by the Republican nominee John McCain whose advertisements clearly spoke to a specific demographic (his core conservative supporters), Obama's advertisements, speeches, and actions invited everyone to come together and work as a unified nation. While John McCain repeatedly said he would not sit down with certain world leaders, Obama wanted to start a dialogue with all world leaders, regardless of current relationships and past events, and move forward together. It was a message of inclusion that American citizens responded to strongly. In the end, the young, inexperienced, African American carried the support of the majority of Americans who voted for the message and promise of inclusion over exclusion.

The Playboy brand message in the 1950s was clear—people should be free to get over their feelings of guilt about sex. In the 1960s, that brand message had grown—people should be free to get over their feelings of guilt about pleasure, whether that pleasure is related to sex, materialism, or anything else. As that brand message evolved, it continued to be inclusive—*everyone* should be able to enjoy the brand promise of *Playboy* (see Box 7.2 for more information about the power of an inclusive brand strategy).

PLAYBOY AS A CULT BRAND

By the 1960s, Playboy had grown into a colossal cult brand (see Box 7.3 for more examples of cult brands). A high level of emotional involvement combined with pervasive publicity and buzz marketing can drive a brand to cult status. Cult brands such as Harley Davidson share one major component in common—they always include a strong level of personalization by consumers. It's that personalization that allows consumers to develop a deep emotional attachment to the brand as

> **BOX 7.3** Cult brands
>
> A cult brand is one that develops a strong following from a group of people who are devoutly loyal to it and search for new ways to experience the brand, and then share those experiences with other members of the group (or cult). Loyalty is derived from a strong emotional connection to the brand.
>
> An example of a cult brand is Ford's Mustang. Mustang owners, who are obsessively loyal to the brand, join Mustang owner clubs, attend Mustang-related events, and purchase Mustang merchandise. Consumers in the cult are drawn together based on their shared emotional involvement in the brand and their desire to experience the brand both personally and together.
>
> Another example is the RIM Blackberry, which is known as the business person's mobile handheld device. Loyal users believe they cannot live without their Blackberries that provide access to email, telephone, the Internet, and more. Members of the Blackberry cult band together as members of the same "club." Even U.S. President Barack Obama is a member of the Blackberry cult. Upon his election in 2008, the U.S. government had to find a way to ensure the president's Blackberry was secure (originally, Obama was told his beloved Blackberry did not meet security requirements), because he refused to give it up. In the minds of Blackberry loyalists, "You're either with us, or against us." The opposite extreme comes from loyal Apple iPhone customers who position their cult of users as very different from but no less important than Blackberry customers. It's an interesting battle, and to date, both brands have developed strongholds in their respective niches.

they relate it and the products under the brand umbrella to their own lives. As established in earlier chapters, every Playboy brand extension allowed consumers to experience the brand and personalize it in new ways. Consumers were given the opportunity to take control of their connections with the brand, which allowed them to develop deep emotional attachments to it.

With each new level of experience with the Playboy brand, consumers could further their emotional connections to it. In other words, consumers moved through the three stages of consumer emotional involvement shown in Figure 7.1: thinking, acting, and feeling. When

A BRAND RISES DESPITE THE NAYSAYERS—THE 1960s

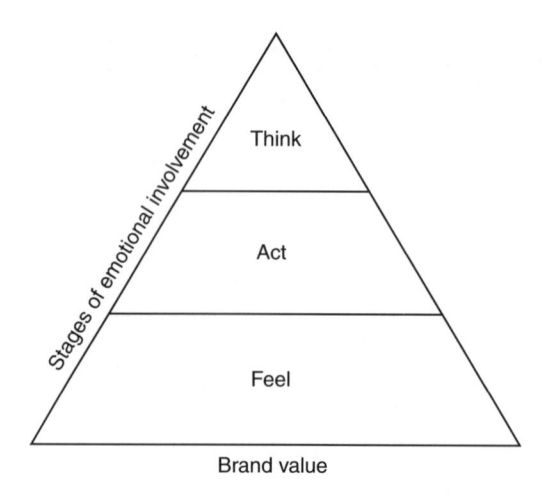

```
                    /\
                   /  \
                  / Think\
                 /--------\
                /   Act    \
               /------------\
              /     Feel     \
             /_____\
                 Brand value
```
Stages of emotional involvement

FIGURE 7.1 **The three stages of consumer emotional involvement**

a consumer first comes into contact with a brand, he is likely to simply interact by *thinking* about the brand. For Playboy consumers, this might include looking at *Playboy* magazine or watching *Playboy After Dark*. As his relationship with the brand evolves, he takes *action* related to it. Playboy consumers could take action by attending the Playboy Jazz Festival or using Playboy branded merchandise. Ultimately, the consumer develops an emotional connection to the brand that causes him to have strong *feelings* toward it. For Playboy consumers, strong feelings were an inevitable by-product of branded experiences such as attending a Playboy Club or visiting a Playboy Resort.

Once strong feelings about a brand are developed, consumers often seek out other people with similar feelings about the brand in order to share those experiences. Human beings are innately social, and all cult brands evolve at the hands of a network of people behind those brands that truly believe in them and want to share them. Playboy began with the belief of Hugh Hefner behind it and grew to attract and convert millions of consumers into believers in the fantasy lifestyle and the brand promise. Watching Hugh Hefner as the living embodiment of the brand made the promise seem much more attainable and touched on a variety of emotional triggers that further connected people to the brand.

As Playboy clubs, resorts, theaters, merchandise, and so on became available, consumers found new ways to extend their relationships with the Playboy brand and with the network of consumers who shared their emotional connection with it. Being a Playboy Club key holder became a status symbol and a symbol of belief in the Playboy message and lifestyle. The cult brand even made an appearance in popular culture when James Bond revealed he was a Playboy Club key holder in the movie *Diamonds Are Forever*. In the case of Playboy, the cult brand took on an exclusivity that mirrored the loyalty of its consumers. That loyalty leads to vocal brand influencers who buy the brand, support the brand, try to convert others to the brand, and defend the brand tirelessly. Playboy represented in the 1960s the kind of brand loyalty brand managers dream of but can rarely manufacture.

Frequently, the rise of a brand to cult status coincides with a time in popular culture where that brand fills a void, allowing customers to fulfill a need. Nowhere is that more true than with Playboy. The brand filled multiple voids and over time evolved to continue to fill new gaps as society changed in terms of personal freedom, self-gratification, equality, liberal political thinking, self-expression, materialism, and more. However, all brands peak at some time. While life was good for Playboy and Hefner in the 1960s, the good times were coming to an end. In just a few short years, everything would change, and this time around, Playboy would not be ready or able to change with the rest of the world.

PART III
A BRAND GOES GLOBAL—THE 1970s

TABLE III **Timeline—The 1970s**

1970: Feminist protesters storm the stage of the *Dick Cavett Show* during an interview with Hugh Hefner. Gloria Steinem publishes an interview with Hugh Hefner in *McCall's* magazine where she compares *Playboy* to Nazi literature. *Penthouse*, which debuted in 1969, began stealing market share from *Playboy*.

1971: Hugh Hefner purchases the Playboy Mansion West in California. Playboy Productions produces Roman Polanski's movie, *Macbeth*. Playboy goes public.

1972: Drug Enforcement Agency opens an investigation against Hugh Hefner and Playboy. *Playboy* circulation peaks at over 7 million copies sold per month. Playboy Enterprises purchases and launches *Oui* magazine.

1973: Playboy pretax income is reported at $20 million.

1974: Hugh Hefner changes *Playboy* pictorials to become more erotic in response to competitive attacks.

1975: Hugh Hefner is exonerated of drug charges. Christie Hefner joins Playboy Enterprises, Inc. The first overseas version of *Playboy* magazine debuts in Germany. Playboy pretax income is reported at $2 million.

1976: The Playboy brand name is removed from the company's New Jersey resort and Chicago hotel. Playboy stock drops to $4 per share. Playboy pretax income is reported at $5 million.

1977: Hugh Hefner hosts *Saturday Night Live*. Playboy Resort in Jamaica closes. Baltimore Playboy Club closes.

1978: New Playboy Casino opens in the Bahamas.

1979: Christie Hefner founds the Playboy Foundation's Hugh M. Hefner Awards. The Playboy Jazz Festival is revived at the Hollywood Bowl. The 25th Anniversary Playmate Reunion is held at the Playboy Mansion West.

CHAPTER 8

THE BRAND SEEN AND PROTESTED AROUND THE WORLD

I enjoy the public's fantasies about the way I live almost as much as I enjoy how much I really live.
　　　　　　　　　Hugh Hefner, Playboy 2000: The Party Continues

As the 1960s, a decade when Americans clashed over numerous social and political issues, came to a close, Playboy found itself with a vision quite unlike the one it had in 1953. No longer dedicated to advocating a specific lifestyle for men, in the 1960s, Playboy advocated liberal thinking and politics while living a life of self-gratification at the same time. As the public rallied around causes related to freedom and equality, Hugh Hefner and Playboy led the way and became more influential, and more controversial, with each passing year. With notoriety, often comes backlash, and Playboy positioned itself to be at the center of that backlash throughout the 1970s.

At the same time, Playboy continued to expand and leverage its popularity and both the positive and negative press behind the brand grew. Most significantly in the 1970s, Playboy made the leap overseas. A global audience was already well aware of Hugh Hefner and Playboy, and they eagerly purchased *Playboy* magazine, visited the international Playboy Clubs, and discussed and shared the controversial, trendsetting, and intriguing brand.

However, the 1970s ushered in a new time of change for Americans and people around the world. The economy was struggling with inflation; unemployment rates were hitting record highs; the government faltered with the resignation of former President Richard Nixon;

> **BOX 8.1** Generation Jones
>
> The members of Generation Jones were born between 1955 and 1964. The oldest members of the generation were children during the 1960s, a time marked with optimism and a shared desire for positive change to human life. They began to reach adulthood during the turbulent 1970s, a time when people struggled financially and economically more than the Baby Boomers Generation had ever experienced at the same age a decade earlier. The changes the Baby Boomers ushered in during the 1960s didn't bring the good times and prosperity that members of Generation Jones expected. As a result, the generation has been characterized as pessimistic and yearning for more than what they found waiting for them when they reached adulthood during the challenging decade of the 1970s.

conflicts around the world affected nearly everyone, particularly the growing Cold War chasm between the United States and the Soviet Union; and life focused more on day-to-day survival for the members of Generation Jones than living the good life and having fun (see Box 8.1 for more information about Generation Jones). That's not to say all was bleak. The disco era kept the party alive, and drugs and sex became more popular as a new spirit of experimentation and rebelliousness set in.

However, macro environmental influences significantly affected the Playboy brand in the 1970s. For example, the Cold War was peaking, the Vietnam War dragged on, and two oil crises directly affected how people lived. The U.S. economy was in dire straits under the worst conditions since the Great Depression. When former President Richard Nixon was impeached and the government was proven to be corrupt, the American people found themselves at the center of complete turmoil politically and economically. Adding to that turmoil was social unrest after desegregation, and racial riots became commonplace. In short, the 1970s were a challenging decade for Americans and people around the world. The changes people asked for in the 1960s were coming, but the results weren't exactly what people expected.

Throughout the turmoil of the 1970s, people searched for ways to escape the problems of the day. Alcohol, drugs, and sex were the prevailing forms of escapism. In a pre-AIDS world, the party lifestyle depicted on the pages of *Playboy* became more alluring than ever, although attaining the fantasy seemed much *less* realistic. When the contraceptive pill became available to unmarried women in 1972, the Playboy lifestyle of sexual liberation grew in popularity, but living the good life in *all* aspects of life was still the ultimate fantasy that seemed to be out of reach. It appeared in the 1970s that Hugh Hefner, the brand champion, was still the only person to be living the dream.

A BRAND ON THE DEFENSIVE

The Playboy fantasy of the 1970s was under attack, and as the decade progressed, the attacks became bigger and louder. Organized protesters began attending events and speaking out against Playboy in larger numbers and more frequently than ever before. Interestingly, many of the protests against Playboy began on college campuses, one of the key target markets for the Playboy brand. In 1972, *Playboy* magazine reached its peak with circulation topping out at over 7 million copies per month, but as the decade progressed, *Playboy's* message of a self-indulgent lifestyle no longer struck the same chord with large numbers of consumers who were struggling to pay bills during the 1970s and rationalize the political, social, and economic unrest of the time.

Perhaps the biggest obstacle facing Playboy in the 1970s was the growing Feminist Movement that directly targeted Playboy and Hugh Hefner as symbols of everything that was keeping women from attaining equality. While Hugh Hefner believed that the Playboy brand's mission was to give liberties to everyone, feminists attacked both Hefner and his Playboy brand as being oppressive to women and exploitative. Truth be told, they weren't that far-off base in many respects.

In the 1950s and 1960s, men dominated society in the United States. Playboy took that dominance a step further and held a distinctly anti-feminist point of view. Hefner admitted in interviews and within the pages of *Playboy* magazine that he did not believe women were equal to men, and he didn't think they should *want* to be equal. He warned men against allowing women to gain too much power. He took a stand stating that society was trying to make women *less* feminine while he and Playboy wanted to *boost* women's femininity. The argument held little validity with the Feminist Movement who organized to attack Hefner and Playboy head-on.

Organized protests by feminists became commonplace in the 1970s where Hugh Hefner and Playboy were concerned. As early as the spring of 1970, feminists tried to make their mark against Playboy in the public eye when two women's rights activists stormed the stage of the popular *Dick Cavett Show* during a televised interview with Hefner. But the feminist attack against Playboy became a national cause in 1970 when now famous feminist journalist Gloria Steinem wrote an article based on an interview with Hugh Hefner that was published in *McCall's* magazine where, among other things, she compared *Playboy* to Nazi literature, drawing the comparison that, "Asking a woman to read *Playboy* was like asking a Jew to read Nazi literature." In 1972, Steinem was named Woman of the Year by *McCall's*.

Hugh Hefner's response would mold the Playboy position on feminism. In interviews and within *Playboy* magazine, Hefner attempted to change his original position. He claimed that Playboy was pro-women's rights but not complete freedom, which he dubbed "radicalism." Rather than support equality completely, Playboy began to refer to feminists as "militant man-haters." The approach resulted in shifting the once highly inclusive brand to an exclusive brand with a message that told consumers, you're either with us or against us. A brand that once told consumers that everyone was invited to the party and could enjoy it together and equally, now told consumers that they could come to the party but there were specific roles to be played and beliefs to support if they wanted to be included. It was a confusing shift in the Playboy brand message that didn't go unnoticed by consumers and fueled the fires of controversy and debate from Playboy protesters.

As the 1970s wore on, Hefner and Playboy backpedaled on the position toward feminism, realizing that excluding the influential group was not helping the brand. Hefner made an attempt in the late 1970s to change his image as a womanizer to an equal rights liberator. He publicly endorsed equal pay and fought for women's liberties. However, the damage had been done. The once omnipotent Hugh Hefner and Playboy had been dubbed hypocritical, and it was true. A negative response to the attack confused consumers' expectations for the brand, and a repositioning strategy that delivered too little, too late, couldn't save Playboy.

A final blow to the Playboy brand came in the early 1970s when the Chicago Playboy Mansion became the center of an ongoing drug investigation. The investigation, which began in 1972, made its way to the press who claimed drugs proliferated the Playboy Mansion and the Hollywood stars who spent time there. The press accused Hugh Hefner of ordering a cover-up when the investigation began and irrevocably harmed both Hefner and Playboy's images significantly.

When the Drug Enforcement Agency arrested Hefner's executive assistant outside of the Chicago Playboy Mansion in 1974 and found drugs in her possession, the drug scandal suddenly carried some truth and the Playboy brand was tarnished. The scandal wouldn't die soon enough for the Playboy brand. In the mid-1970s, several more Playboy employees were arrested on drug charges. Although Hugh Hefner denies ever doing hard drugs and no evidence was ever found against him, the damage had been done, and Playboy was directly linked to the drug culture of the 1970s in consumers' eyes. It didn't help, of course, that Hefner had publicly advocated marijuana use in the past, citing it as another personal freedom people ought to have.

Hefner paid all of his executive assistant's legal bills, but on January 12, 1975, she committed suicide from a drug and alcohol overdose. Hefner immediately held a press conference where he attacked the government, calling the investigation a "witch hunt" and politically motivated in order to tarnish both his reputation and the Playboy brand. He positioned himself and Playboy as the victims, and the court of public opinion began to feel sympathy for him. In 1975, the drug case was dropped against Hefner, and the head of the Drug Enforcement Agency resigned. A public statement was issued stating no evidence had ever been found against Hefner, but the damage to the Playboy brand would not be forgotten anytime soon. In the end, macro environmental factors shaped another phase of the Playboy brand lifecycle and directly affected the company's bottom line as sales of *Playboy* magazine began to fall in record numbers.

PLAYBOY GOES GLOBAL

As the 1970s passed and backlash against Hugh Hefner and the Playboy brand grew, the brand managed to survive. When the decade had opened, Playboy found itself without a brand guardian. Hugh Hefner, who had once agonized over every detail of the magazine, brand and business, now withdrew from day-to-day operations. His focus moved from business to celebrity. He purchased a new home in California, Playboy Mansion West, and spent less and less time in Chicago. He still defined the brand goals and was the face of the brand, but his employees ran company operations. With no brand guardian, no clear positioning, and no focus, the company faltered.

In 1971, Playboy went public as Playboy Enterprises, Inc. to much excitement and making Hugh Hefner one of the wealthiest self-made entrepreneurs in history, but that enthusiasm would be short-lived. At the time, *Playboy* was peaking with magazine circulation at over 7 million copies per month (responsible for half of the company's 1970 revenue of $132 million and most of the company's net income of $9.2 million), 23 clubs, resorts, hotels, and casinos with nearly 1 million members worldwide. Throughout the decade, Playboy's stock price was volatile as the brand struggled against protesters, a drug scandal, and a weak economy in the United States. Even the 1974, 20th anniversary celebration couldn't save the struggling brand and company.

By 1975, *Playboy* magazine experienced one of the largest reader losses in magazine history when its circulation numbers dropped by nearly 20% from a peak of 7 million in 1972 to 5.8 million 3 years later. In 1975, Playboy guaranteed advertisers a circulation rate of 6 million, which wasn't being met. As a result, the company was forced to extend credits to advertisers, and ad revenue dropped by 7.6%. At the same time, advertisers began to pull out amid the controversy and drug scandals Playboy faced in the mid-1970s, and a company that once turned all it touched to gold, now struggled to find itself. All focus had been lost.

The brand, which included book publishing, merchandising, a modeling agency, a limousine service, a record label, a television and movie company, resorts, clubs, casinos, and more, was too big to sustain itself, and something had to change. As early as 1970, Playboy Clubs were faltering, and Playboy hotel operations were losing money. However, *Playboy* magazine was still strong. Hugh Hefner invested approximately $30 million on a new resort in New Jersey and another $3 million on financing Roman Polanski's film adaptation of *Macbeth*. Clearly, business decisions were still being made based more on Hefner's interests than long-term growth strategies.

It could be argued that what saved the Playboy brand in the 1970s was globalization. As technology and communication across borders increased, the world shrank, and Playboy found a new audience outside the United States. In 1972, the first overseas edition of *Playboy* magazine debuted in Germany with other international editions premiering in Australia, Brazil, Japan, and Mexico during the same decade. The London Playboy Club and Casino was thriving and Playboy Clubs were operating in the Philippines, Jamaica (also a resort), and Montreal. The 1970s brought new Playboy Clubs to the United Kingdom (Portsmouth and Manchester) and Japan (Tokyo, Osaka, and Nagoya) and a new casino to the Bahamas. Expansion outside the United States was fast and profitable in the 1970s as the Playboy brand mystique and the world's interest in the brand champion, Hugh Hefner's, life spread across the globe thanks to the frenzied press and controversy that surrounded both the man and the brand.

Brand buzz is a powerful thing. It can drive short-term results, but sustaining that buzz to drive long-term growth requires focused strategy. The problem for Playboy was that international expansion couldn't solve the core problems of the company, and after peaking in 1972, the company and the brand began to suffer. Add new competition to the impacts of the macro environment and Playboy was not ready for the downturn in business that the latter half of the 1970s would bring.

CHAPTER 9

A BRAND PEAKS

I didn't want to end up imitating the imitators.
Hugh Hefner December 2008 Interview with Askmen.com about his feelings related to competitor attacks in the 1970s

In 1972, Playboy reached the height of its popularity. *Playboy* magazine enjoyed circulation of over 7 million copies per month and was positioned as the leading men's magazine as well as one of the most influential magazines in the world. Dozens of Playboy clubs, casinos, hotels, and resorts were operating profitably with nearly 1 million members. The brand had expanded into various markets and categories including merchandising, television and movie producing, record producing, modeling and limousine services, and more. The writing was on the wall for a long time that the growth of the Playboy brand could not be sustained, but steps were never taken to protect the company from an inevitable crash.

In 1972, Playboy was still being referred to as an empire with limitless potential, but within a very short amount of time, the applause would die and Playboy would be attacked for mismanagement and a lack of business strategy experience. Hugh Hefner had removed himself from the day-to-day operations of the company by 1970. While he remained in the public eye as the ultimate brand champion and physical embodiment of the brand promise, he was absent from company operations. His focus moved to his celebrity status, his role as the brand champion, and living the brand promise. He still controlled major business decisions, but he was absent from operational management.

Instead, he purchased a new home, Playboy Mansion West, in an exclusive section of Beverly Hills, California, and immersed himself in the celebrity lifestyle he idolized since his childhood. With his Big Bunny DC-9 Jet, *Playboy After Dark* television series and more money than he could spend, Hefner was living the Playboy fantasy in every way.

At the same time, Playboy as a company began to struggle. After Playboy went public in 1971, profits began to drop quickly. The macro environment took a toll on Playboy. Americans struggled financially and politically, and the drug investigations discussed in Chapter 8 directly impacted sales of *Playboy* magazine and the brand image overall in the minds of consumers. A number of restructurings were ordered in an attempt to bring in a strong management team who could turn the business around before it was too late. However, with a lack of focus still missing from the business strategy, the effort ended up being too little too late, and profits dipped to dangerously low levels. In 1973, pretax profit was reported at $20 million, but by 1975, pretax profit had fallen to just $2 million. By 1976, Playboy company stock hit a low of just $4 per share.

COMPETITIVE ATTACKS AGAINST THE PIONEER BRAND

In 1969, consumers started to see ads for a new men's magazine, *Penthouse*. The new publication attacked *Playboy* directly and arrogantly. Much of the concepts used in *Penthouse* were copied from the pages of *Playboy* without apology, including features, titles, and so on. *Penthouse* debuted in England in 1965, but the new decade would bring it to the United States. With a brand message that labeled *Playboy* as lagging behind the times, *Penthouse* positioned itself as the men's magazine for a new generation. The content was far more sexually explicit than what consumers found in the pages of *Playboy*, which differentiated it just far enough from the pioneer brand, *Playboy*, to give it immediate attention (see Box 9.1 for more information about competitive market positioning strategies).

Initially, Hefner ordered his staff to ignore *Penthouse*, but as they watched sales of the new competitor's magazine skyrocket from 235,000 for the first issue published in the United States in September 1969 to 2 million copies by mid-1972, it could no longer be ignored. Quickly, *Penthouse* was stealing market share from *Playboy* and converting consumers to believe the *Penthouse* messages that *Playboy* wasn't keeping up with the times and consumers' needs from a men's

BOX 9.1   Competitive market positioning strategies

Marketers typically define four primary competitive market-positioning strategies:

- *Market leader*: As the name implies, the market leader position is the one on top with the biggest market share and the most strength. *Playboy* was the market leader and the pioneer brand (the first in the market), which gave it immense strength leading up to the 1970s. Another example is McDonald's as the market leader in the U.S. fast food restaurant industry.

- *Market challenger*: Companies in the market challenger position try to directly and aggressively steal market share from the market leader. Both *Penthouse* and *Hustler* were market challengers in the 1970s. Unfortunately, the Playboy company's *Oui* magazine was also a market challenger to the market leader. Similarly, Burger King is the market challenger to McDonald's as the market leader. By differentiating its food as flame-broiled rather than fried and directly attacking McDonald's since its inception in 1954 (14 years after McDonald's debuted), Burger King has always followed a strategy of aggressively attempting to steal market share from McDonald's. Today, Burger King is the second largest fast food chain in the United States, behind McDonald's.

- *Market follower*: Companies in the market follower position don't want to risk directly challenging the market leader. Instead, these companies are satisfied with stealing away customers who are dissatisfied with both the market leader and challengers and are looking for an alternative. Wendy's could be defined as a market follower within the fast food industry. While Wendy's has made clear attempts to differentiate its brand from the market leader and market challengers (think of the famous "Where's the beef?" campaign in the United States in the 1980s), its focus has been on stealing customers who have specific problems with the products and services offered by the market leader and challengers. Today, Wendy's (which debuted in 1969) is the third largest fast food restaurant chain in the United States.

- *Market nichers*: Companies in the market nicher position are small and typically meaningless to the market leader. These companies occupy a very small space in the marketplace and don't present a

> threat to larger competitors. They typically focus efforts on a select few target markets. A company like Hardee's could be considered a market nicher in the fast food restaurant industry. Hardee's focuses on being known as a niche hamburger chain that concentrates on building a presence in smaller towns where larger fast-food chains don't invest, particularly in the Midwest and Southeast regions of the United States. Hardee's position as market nicher is strong. Since its debut in 1960, Hardee's has grown to be the fourth largest fast food chain in the United States. Alternately, Boston Market, which was launched in 1985, could be considered a market nicher simply because of its focus on delivering healthier food (particularly fresh chicken products) quickly.

magazine were accurate. The first counterattack from *Playboy* (see Box 9.2 for details about offensive and defensive positioning strategies) came in the form of a new, more explicitly pornographic magazine. In 1972, Hefner purchased *Oui* magazine from a French publisher through Playboy Enterprises. *Oui* was an established publication in France with more sexually explicit content than Hefner published in *Playboy*, and he believed that by acquiring a magazine that competed directly with *Penthouse*, he could beat *Penthouse's* owner, Robert Guccione, at his own game. However, the plan backfired. Rather than steal market share back from *Penthouse*, *Oui* succeeded only in shifting a portion of Playboy Enterprises' share of the men's magazine market from *Playboy* to *Oui*.

In 1976, sales of *Penthouse* reached between 4.5 to 5 million, while *Playboy* circulation had dropped from its peak of 7 million copies per month down to between 5 and 6 million copies per month. While *Playboy* failed to meet guaranteed circulation numbers for advertisers month after month, *Penthouse* raised its circulation guarantee to advertisers by half a million. In short, Playboy's strategies and tactics to thwart competitors in the 1970s were completely reactive and unsuccessful.

Another competing men's magazine, *Hustler*, was released in 1974. Although its content was far more hard-core pornographic than both *Playboy* and *Penthouse*, the magazine did succeed in stealing market share from the category leaders, and at its peak, *Hustler's* circulation hit 3 million copies per month. In a second attempt to counterattack *Penthouse* and other competitors, Hefner made the decision to

BOX 9.2   Offensive and defensive positioning strategies

Marketers generally follow three primary offensive positioning strategies and four primary defensive positioning strategies that can be directly applied to the competitive environment surrounding *Playboy* in the 1970s.

Offensive Positioning Strategies

Frontal attack: The market challenger directly attacks the market leader in its core market. Both *Penthouse* and *Hustler* used frontal attack strategies to attack *Playboy* in the 1970s.

Flanking attack: The market challenger finds and exploits the market leader's weakness in order to steal market share. Apple has used this strategy successfully in recent years as it attacked the vulnerabilities (such as a greater propensity to acquire viruses) of the market leader, Microsoft Windows.

Guerrilla attack: The market challenger uses a series of small and ongoing tactics in order to frustrate or hinder the market leader and raise awareness of the market challenger within specific market segments. The market leader is unlikely to see a small attack from a seemingly insignificant competitor as a serious threat, but if those attacks can be sustained, they can ultimately have a significant impact on the success of the small market challenger. Mozilla's Firefox Internet browser is a good example of a brand that successfully used a guerrilla attack strategy against the market leader, Microsoft Internet Explorer.

Defensive Positioning Strategies

Position defense: The market leader introduces a range of products to create a defensive barrier around its brand and keep competitors out. In simplest terms, market challengers have difficulty finding gaps to fill or opportunities to break through the market leader's line of defense.

Pre-emptive defense: To thwart an imminent attack, the market leader can launch its own offensive tactics to counter the attack and negate its effects. Google, with its wide variety of online applications,

> products, and services, is a great example of a brand that uses the position defense strategy. Playboy tried this defensive strategy with the acquisition of *Oui*.
>
> Counter-offensive defense: The market leader responds to a market challenger's attack with an even greater attack of its own, which the smaller challenger cannot respond to adequately.
>
> Strategic withdrawal: When a market leader overextends its brand and resources, the time ultimately comes when a strategic withdrawal from underperforming ventures becomes a necessity so focus can be put back on the most valuable assets. The Playboy company found itself in this defensive position in the 1970s.

reposition *Playboy* again. The magazine that advocated tasteful sexual freedom now moved to become more erotic with more explicitly pornographic pictorials. The battle of explicit photos between *Penthouse* and *Playboy* was dubbed the Pubic Wars in the 1970s as the brands competed by pushing the envelope of accepted decency further and further. However, *Playboy* consumers, who had long associated the brand with a positive, classy, and indulgent lifestyle, were confused by what many referred to as a shift from eroticism to obscenity.

Of course, the controversy surrounding the Pubic Wars and the competition between *Playboy* and *Penthouse* would fuel the buzz about both brands and provide awareness and interest in them, but it also clouded the Playboy brand promise. One of the keys to successful brand building is consistency in messaging. When *Playboy* magazine shifted its product from eroticism to more explicit pornography, loyal consumers' demands were not necessarily met. As a brand develops over time, consistent messaging and continually delivering on the brand promise creates expectations in consumers' minds derived from the three core factors of building customer loyalty, called the Three Ss of Customer Loyalty:

1. *Stability:* Customers become loyal to a product when that product (or brand) sends a consistent message.
2. *Sustainability*: Customers become loyal to a product when they expect that product (or brand) to be with them for a long period of time or at least a specific amount of time with a clearly defined end.

3. *Security*: Customers become loyal to a product when that product (or brand) gives them a feeling of comfort or piece of mind.

Since its debut in 1953, *Playboy* magazine represented a high quality, free lifestyle that men aspired to achieve. The content may have evolved over the course of its first 20 years in existence, but consumers felt stable in the core consistent message of living a specific type of life. At the same time, customers knew that their next issue of *Playboy* magazine would come at a specific time each month without fail. The magazine's subscriber numbers made up the vast majority of *Playboy* sales, demonstrating that customers wanted to have a long, sustained relationship with the brand. Furthermore, customers felt secure with the Playboy brand. Month after month, the product delivered on a consistent brand message and value proposition—living the good life people deserve. The features of the magazine stayed similar throughout the 20-year life of the brand, and consumers felt comfortable in knowing what to expect from *Playboy*.

However, in the mid-1970s, Playboy made a desperate, reactive decision to completely change the Playboy image in order to directly compete with challengers like *Penthouse* and *Hustler*. It was a bold decision that the company felt would keep the magazine relevant in consumers' minds. With the new proliferation of sexual material throughout various markets and categories in the 1970s, Playboy made a decision that completely contradicted its brand image and succumbed to competitive pressures. While the new, more sexually explicit images that now appeared in *Playboy* may have appealed to some existing consumers and some new customers, there were a large number of loyal customers who were left confused by the change. Loyal customers who had strong expectations for the Playboy brand suddenly didn't know what to expect anymore. The result was an even greater loss in circulation numbers for *Playboy* magazine (see Box 9.3 for more examples of brands that shifted direction and confused consumers).

Customer confusion wasn't the only negative result of *Playboy's* shift to become more sexually explicit. Advertisers were equally confused and exited quickly and in droves. Hefner's goal had been to try to ensure *Playboy* stayed relevant based on the success *Penthouse* was experiencing and the obvious market for more sexually explicit content. However, consumers and advertisers weren't prepared for the pioneer brand to change in order to compete directly with its smaller competitor.

> **BOX 9.3** Brands that failed to meet customer expectations
>
> The Coca-Cola Company released a product in April 1985 that went down in history as one of the worst brand strategies ever developed. That product was called New Coke, and it was developed to compete directly with Pepsi, which was quickly gaining market share at the time in the competitive soft drink market. New Coke was launched with a different taste than consumers expected from Coke. Had Coca-Cola simply released New Coke as a brand extension, it may have worked (although, one could argue it would have done little more than take market share from Coke), however, Coca-Cola introduced New Coke as a replacement to a product that consumers were already very loyal to. They had expectations for Coke, and New Coke didn't fulfill them. Coke returned to the market just 3 months after New Coke was released.
>
> Another example of a brand that failed to meet customer expectations is Saturn. When the company began losing money in the late 1990s and 2000s, General Motors took steps to cut many of the differentiators that customers had come to expect from the Saturn brand. Suddenly, "a different kind of company, a different kind of car," looked very similar to all the other brands on the market. The brand promise was confused and consumers simply didn't believe it anymore. As a result, a brand that stood for something quite different from any other auto company in the early 1990s became indistinguishable from other brands on the market.

The pioneer brand, as category leader, had made a mistake, and Hefner realized it. In 1975, he ordered a return to *Playboy*'s original brand vision to make sex and nudity acceptable in American society without the guilt and repression he experienced during his youth. *Playboy* returned to its core mission of being a men's lifestyle magazine that also included sexual images and content. Articles refocused on romanticism and living the free lifestyle that *Playboy* had advocated for two decades before. A new advertising campaign launched in 1977 to announce *Playboy*'s return to the magazine's roots as a purveyor of information, ideas, and inspiration to live a specific, fantasy lifestyle.

However, *Playboy*'s competition in the 1970s did not come from the publishing industry alone. As the 1970s passed, *Playboy* would face competition from a variety of sources as sex became less taboo and more mainstream. Sex shops, strip clubs, sex-related books, pornographic movies, and more became commonplace across the United States, and consumers from all walks of life had access to these products in multiple forms. Even though Hugh Hefner had argued since *Playboy* debuted in 1953 that it wasn't a sex magazine but rather was a men's lifestyle magazine, much of the consumer public associated the brand with sex, particularly since Hefner's busy sex life had become fodder for the press. The new availability of sex through so many products, categories, and experiences made *Playboy* less mysterious than it was in decades earlier, and *Playboy* struggled to find its relevancy in a sexually liberated, economically downtrodden society. In short, Playboy and Hugh Hefner were victims of their own success. The causes Hefner fought for during the 1950s and 1960s were won (or at least close to being won), and the Playboy brand no longer had a clear market position, message, or identity.

SIGNS OF BRAND TROUBLE BECOME A REALITY

Hugh Hefner's decision in 1975 to reposition *Playboy* back to its roots and away from the pornography of competitors was a step in the right direction to save the Playboy brand, but it wouldn't be enough. For decades, the Playboy brand had been overextended, and brand expansion without restraint can never be sustained (see Box 9.4 for another example of brand expansion without restraint).

By the mid-1970s, *Playboy* magazine was still profitable, but many Playboy Clubs were losing money and the Playboy-owned hotels and resorts were floundering. The first big movie produced by Playboy Productions, Roman Polanski's *Macbeth*, was critically acclaimed but a box office disaster. In 1973, Playboy Enterprises enjoyed pretax profits of $20 million, but by 1975, that number had dropped to an abysmal $2 million. The company had grown with little focus, and by the mid-1970s, virtually every aspect of the business was losing money except *Playboy* magazine and the London Playboy Club and Casino. In fact, the Playboy Clubs, once deemed the ultimate Playboy brand experience, were losing the most money during the economic slowdown of the 1970s, and the $30 million resort built in New Jersey during the previous decade had yet to break even.

In 1975, a task force was put together to make recommendations to Hefner on how to save Playboy. By 1976, a restructuring was in place, with a new chief operating officer, Victor Lownes (a confidant of Hugh

BOX 9.4 Brand expansion without restraint

In 1983, the first Hooters restaurant opened in Florida. Today, there are over 400 Hooters franchise restaurants in 43 states and nearly 30 countries and territories around the world. The Hooters company does not try to hide that its brand promise is good food with good-looking women. On the "About" page on the Hooters.com Web site, visitors are told, "Sex appeal is legal and it sells." The description goes on to say, "Hooters marketing, emphasizing the Hooters Girl and her sex appeal, along with its commitment to quality operations continues to build and contributes to the chain's success. Hooters' business motto sums it up, 'you can sell the sizzle, but you have to deliver the steak.'" Hooters makes no apology for its reliance on feminine sexuality to sell its products. The Web site's "About" page clearly states, "The company has no plans to alter the concept and feels doing so would be a tremendous disservice to its franchisees, employees, and customers."

The Hooters brand message and promise is crystal clear. Brand extensions such as Hooters girl calendars, a Miss Hooters International competition, a Hooters-branded MasterCard Rewards program (users earn points which can be applied to purchases at Hooters locations), and Hooters T-shirts and clothing, all work to further that brand promise. A number of professional sports sponsorships such as golf, car-racing, powerboat racing, and a motorcycle team also appealed to the target audience and aligned with their expectations for the brand.

However, in the 2000s, Hooters ventured into new businesses outside of the company's core competencies. The brand began to expand without necessary restraint and consumers were introduced to Hooters Air in 2003 and a Hooters Energy Drink in 2007. Both failed to meet customer expectations for the Hooters brand, and did little more than confuse customers who couldn't make the connection between a Hooters airline, a Hooters energy drink, and the Hooters brand promise of good food and good-looking women. The leap was just too big, and both products failed quickly.

In addition, Hooters entered the Las Vegas hotel and casino market in 2006. This is another business the company had little knowledge of or experience with, and it showed. By 2008, cash flow was falling and an investment group attempted to purchase the property from Hooters. The deal fell through, but the future remains uncertain for

A BRAND GOES GLOBAL—THE 1970s

> the Hooters Casino Hotel. Just as Playboy made many attempts to ride the wave of its popular brand by expanding the brand far and wide, Hooters has made errors in expanding its brand with a lack of restraint. The writing was on the wall in 2000 when in an interview with CNN/Money about Hooters' plans to purchase the bankrupt Vanguard Airlines, Hooters vice president of marketing, Mike McNeil said, "The first step is to assess if there's a desire to get in this business, what it's going to take to get these guys back up in the air, trying to understand the business, because quite frankly we don't understand it very well yet." It's not surprising that Hooters Air closed in 2006 after just 3 years in operation. When a brand strays too far from its core promise and consumers can't make the necessary connections between extensions and their expectations for the brand, those extensions are likely to fail and the company and brand suffer.

Hefner), and a plan to refocus the company. Lownes quickly acquired the nickname of "Ax Man" among the ranks of Playboy employees after he swiftly cut the company's budget to operate Playboy hotels and clubs by more than 35%. Lownes discontinued the *VIP* magazine for Playboy Club key holders and cut 50 people from the Playboy staff. One highly visible change for Playboy employee morale came when Lownes dismissed the entire "Bunny department" who had kept updated files and status records on every Playboy bunny in the United States. Even Hugh Hefner, himself, was not spared from Lownes' corporate cost-cutting tactics. The black Big Bunny Jet DC-9, an iconic symbol of the Playboy brand promise, was sold, and the Chicago Playboy Mansion was all but closed.

Victor Lownes did not believe that Hugh Hefner's lifestyle and celebrity were valuable to Playboy anymore. Instead, his focus was entirely on retaining profits through drastic and rapid cost-cutting measures. Lownes restructured Playboy's business model from running its various businesses centrally to pursuing licensing and franchising deals. He loosened the strict rules at Playboy clubs and hotels related to consistently presenting the Playboy brand and encouraged managers to redesign the clubs as they saw fit. Taking that idea a step further, he eliminated the rule that forbade Playboy Club Bunnies from dating guests. Lownes even removed the Playboy name from the company's hotels in Chicago and New Jersey. The only area of business Lownes did not have authority over was *Playboy* magazine, which Hefner continued to control with a tight grip.

The restructuring coincided with an article in the *Wall Street Journal* that reported a bleak future for Playboy, stating the magazine was suffering from a drop in circulation and advertising, the record and movie divisions were losing money, and the hotels, resorts, and U.S. Playboy Clubs were operating in the red. Perhaps most eye-opening to the public was the report in the *Wall Street Journal* article that Playboy had lost two bank lines of credit worth $6.5 million during the drug scandal of the mid-1970s. With all forces seemingly at work against Playboy in 1975, the company entered 1976 with a new corporate structure and a goal to create the brand focus that had been missing from the business strategy for so long.

The first step to saving Playboy in the mid-1970s was defining the brand focus discussed in Chapter 5. In early 1976, Playboy Enterprises deemed the Playboy brand name to be a detriment to some of its business endeavors. In order to attract a broader audience, including conservative business conventions, the Playboy brand name was removed from its New Jersey resort and Chicago hotel. By mid-1977, the strategy turned to trimming the fat—eliminating the business endeavors that were not working and the company had neither little knowledge of nor experience in. The Playboy Resort in Jamaica was closed as was the Baltimore Playboy Club, symbolizing the start of a string of closures that would take place in the years to come. The Playboy theaters were sold as were the record and movie divisions. In September 1977, Playboy Enterprises laid off 70 employees, and the company turned a modest profit in both 1977 and 1978, thanks to the continued success of the magazine and the London casino.

The gaming industry was the new cash cow for Playboy in the late 1970s, and as the money continued to roll in from the London casino, the company moved to open a second casino in the Bahamas in 1978, and construction began in 1979 on a $135 million hotel and casino in Atlantic City, New Jersey. Unfortunately, gaming wasn't Playboy's core competency nor was it Playboy's focus. At a time when the brand should have been focusing on contraction, it was expanding further into an area that was outside of its expertise. It's not surprising that just a few years later Playboy's casinos would come crashing down.

In the late 1970s though, the focus was on the short-term profits the casinos brought in with little regard to long-term strategy. It's a trap the company fell into again and again during the first three decades of the Playboy brand, but despite the inconsistent branding decisions at the corporate level in the 1970s and the lack of brand restraint that existed since the brand debuted in 1953, one thing remained constant—Hugh Hefner as the ultimate brand champion, and his celebrity status, continued to rise regardless of the Playboy company's performance. He was the best promotional piece a brand could have, and Hefner and the people at Playboy Enterprises knew it.

CHAPTER 10

A BRAND SEES THE ERROR OF ITS WAYS AND TRIES TO GIVE BACK

Brand is only permission to play. It's not a guarantee of success.
Christie Hefner in a 1999 interview
with ContextMag

In February 1970, Hugh Hefner's private DC-9 jet, named Big Bunny, took off on its inaugural flight from Chicago to Los Angeles. On board were a crew of Jet Bunnies and ten reporters in addition to the Playboy brand champion and a bevy of friends. The Playboy lifestyle had grown so big that the ground could no longer support it, and the party took to the sky. Inside the plane, a Playboy Club was born. The plane was designed to look like a flying apartment with a disco area, game area, movie area, music, food, drinks, and women. At a time when very few companies used private jets and even fewer individuals owned one, Big Bunny represented the epitome of extravagance, and it was just the first step in Hugh Hefner's quest to position himself as a successful celebrity living the Playboy fantasy.

As early as the late 1950s, Hefner made a conscious decision to live the brand he created. He purposely changed his shy personality to be more extroverted, purchased a Mercedes-Benz 300SL, and began smoking a pipe and wearing pajamas to add to his mystique and the mystique of the Playboy brand. In the early 1970s, Hefner had extricated himself from the daily workings of the Playboy company and focused more time than ever on his public persona. When *Playboy After Dark* premiered, Hefner used Big Bunny to fly back and forth from Chicago to Los Angeles where the program was filmed on a Hollywood set.

As Hefner's new television show took on a Hollywood appearance, so did Hefner, and so did the Playboy brand. It's not surprising Hefner would be attracted to the Hollywood celebrity lifestyle. He has stated in countless interviews that since his childhood, he used movies to escape his repressed upbringing, and the allure continued throughout his adult life.

On February 3, 1971, Hefner purchased a new home, so he could spend more time in Hollywood, which he came to enjoy more and more. For over $1 million, Hefner purchased Playboy Mansion West (at the time, the largest real estate transaction in Los Angeles history), and after extensive renovations inspired by a recent trip to Africa, he dubbed it Disneyland for adults. The official opening of Playboy Mansion West was held as a fundraiser for the ACLU. The new mansion represented a constant party and grew to become an icon of self-gratification and extravagance unto itself. By 1975, Hefner was completely entrenched in the Hollywood lifestyle and moved permanently to Playboy Mansion West. He used the mansion as a tool to reinvent himself again in the 1970s and played the role of ladies man to the hilt, much to the admonition of members of the Feminist Movement but much to the appreciation of Playboy brand followers.

By the late 1970s, Hefner had become the ultimate icon of the Playboy brand promise. He appeared on *Saturday Night Live* in 1977, making him accessible to a new audience and solidifying his place as a major celebrity. He also allowed several specials for ABC-TV to be filmed at the mansion in the late 1970s, and he spent time working to restore the Hollywood sign in Los Angeles, California. He later received a star on the Hollywood Walk of Fame for his efforts. At the same time, he continued to receive awards and recognition for his ongoing fight for freedom of speech and equality (see Box 10.1 for a list of awards Hefner received during the 1970s).

In simplest terms, the world of business was never Hefner's primary interest, and in the 1970s, he decided to live the life he always wanted with no restrictions. He took it upon himself to be not just the Playboy brand champion but to live the lifestyle to the ultimate extreme. After all, if he couldn't live the Playboy life, then who could? In the 1970s, Hefner's reputation and celebrity grew so much that people either idolized him or loathed him. There was little middle ground, and the publicity and controversy surrounding the man, the magazine, and the company simply fueled the buzz and added to the brand mystique.

> **BOX 10.1** Awards and honors bestowed upon Hugh Hefner during the 1970s
>
> (Adapted from PlayboyEnterprises.com)
>
> - **1971**: ACLU of Southern California names Hugh Hefner Man of the Year.
> - **1974**: Hugh Hefner is honored for his "profound influence on legislative and judicial thought" by the San Fernando Criminal Bar Association.
> - **1976**: Hugh Hefner is named publisher of the year by the Pacific Coast Independent Magazine Wholesalers Association.
> - **1977**: Hugh Hefner receives a "special humanitarian award" from the Beverly Hills-Hollywood Chapter of the NAACP.
> - **1978**: Los Angeles, California Mayor Tom Bradley declares December 4 Hugh M. Hefner Day.
> - **1978**: Hugh Hefner serves as the honorary chairman of the 11th annual NAACP Image Awards at the Los Angeles Century City Plaza.

As Hugh Hefner concentrated on himself in the 1970s, taking the Playboy brand promise to the extreme, Playboy Enterprises suffered. The court of public opinion was again mixed with regard to Hugh Hefner and the Playboy brand. While many saw him as an influential leader and agent of change for civil liberty, others saw him as a symbol of extravagance that didn't resonate with the economic struggles Americans were facing around him. He was labeled as irresponsible for advocating a lifestyle of personal gratification while most Americans were struggling financially and facing rising divorce rates, drug abuse, racial riots, illegitimate births, and venereal disease. The societal unrest of the macro environment seemed to many people to be completely lost on Hugh Hefner and the Playboy brand. As the 1970s progressed, much of the content of *Playboy* magazine started to focus on Hefner and his life, and some consumers could no longer relate to a lifestyle that seemed so far out of reach. As a result, sales of *Playboy* magazine began to fall and the brand and company faced one new challenge after another as they struggled to stay alive in the 1970s.

CHANGING COURSE AND SAVING FACE THROUGH BRAND BUILDING

As the 1970s passed, the Playboy brand was losing relevance, market share, and money. As discussed in Chapter 9, a corporate restructuring and renewed focus on core competencies helped drive profits back into the black, but efforts also had to be taken to re-energize the brand; never before had the company been faced with challenges of rebuilding the brand. From the beginning, the Playboy brand had grown like wildfire with nothing standing in its way. In the 1970s, the world had changed, consumers had changed, and the marketplace had changed. Playboy had extended in more markets and categories than it could sustain and something had to give. The brand had reached its peak, and was forced to contract in order to slowdown its path down the dark side of the product lifecycle.

In 1975, Hugh Hefner convinced his daughter, Christie, to join Playboy Enterprises with the hope that she would one day accept a role as heir apparent to the Playboy empire. It was a step in the right direction as far as Hefner was concerned to keep control of the Playboy brand without being directly involved in the daily operations of the company. If his daughter took over the company one day, he would have eyes and ears in the Chicago office that he trusted and could help keep his company on track without his close involvement.

Although Playboy went public in 1971, Hefner was still the majority shareholder and led all major decisions. A restructuring in 1975 worked to control and improve the micro environment of Playboy, but little could be done to affect the macro environment beyond the existing work Hefner and Playboy did supporting equal rights, civil liberties, and so on. Hefner couldn't change the economy. He couldn't make the oil crises go away, and he couldn't fix a faltering government. Instead, efforts were made to build the brand back up again in the eyes of consumers from the inside.

The Playboy Mansion West became the venue for many political events throughout the 1970s, and television specials were filmed in an attempt to remind consumers that Playboy stood not only for excess and materialism but also for fun and freedom. In 1979, the Playboy Jazz Festival was revived at the Hollywood Bowl in California and became bigger and better than ever, allowing everyday people to experience the brand again. The same year, 136 former Playmates gathered at Playboy Mansion West for a Playmate Reunion. The enthusiasm and publicity around the Playmate Reunion brought a new positive buzz and excitement to the brand that hadn't been present in quite awhile.

Perhaps most significantly in the 1970s, Christie Hefner founded the Playboy Foundation's Hugh M. Hefner Awards in 1979 to honor individuals who make significant contributions in protecting and enhancing First Amendment rights for Americans. The awards program helped to reposition the Playboy brand as being interested in more than self-gratification and reminded consumers that Hugh Hefner and Playboy meant more than sex and excess.

FACING A SEGMENTED MARKET

As the 1970s neared an end, Playboy was faced with a segmented market that it wasn't prepared to handle. Until this time, the brand succeeded by providing a variety of experiential products to consumers and allowing them to control those products and personalize them. In the 1970s, external influences such as the macro environment and new competition would force the market to segment itself organically. People changed, society changed, and the Playboy consumer market changed. Its niche had grown and by necessity split into smaller groups or subniches with varied wants and needs for the brand. Playboy was not prepared to recognize and adapt to a segmented marketing strategy.

When *Penthouse* debuted in 1969 and immediately began to steal market share from *Playboy* magazine, it was clear that the frontal attack was working and a segment of *Playboy* customers were going to shift to the new product that was better able to meet their specific changing needs. Playboy's ill-conceived attempts to counter the attack lacked in long-term strategy and focused instead on short-term tactics. Rather than analyzing the changing market and creating demographic and behavioral segmentation strategies, Playboy jumped to make changes that failed to achieve the objectives expected. Instead, core consumers were confused, advertisers were outraged, and the reactionary tactics delivered negative results.

Had a cluster analysis been conducted in the early 1970s, customers could have been grouped based on similar characteristics and measurable objectives could have been defined for each segment with effective marketing tactics developed accordingly to meet those objectives. To describe further, a cluster analysis is a technique used to organically segment customers based on existing characteristics. Those characteristics can be based on demographic and behavioral traits. The goal of a cluster analysis is to group customers so all members of a specific group are as similar to each other as possible. By nature of the process, each *group* will be distinctively different from the next. In other words, a cluster analysis allows marketers to separate customers into unique segments with unique needs, wants, and expectations.

Segmentation allows marketers to create targeted messaging and positioning and create strategies that meet both short- and long-term objectives related to those specific segments. Rather than using an all or nothing approach, a segmented approach would identify gaps, opportunities, and threats allowing Playboy to focus on the most profitable segments and maximize return on investments. Unfortunately, that's a strategy the company wouldn't recognize or fully employ for many more years.

During the 1970s, Playboy still acted on many of Hugh Hefner's whims. The brand champion had extricated himself from the daily operations of Playboy Enterprises, but he still controlled major decisions. That disconnect, and an overall lack of long-term strategic thinking, would make it impossible for Playboy to redefine itself and reposition its iconic brand in the 1970s. Unfortunately, the worst was yet to come. The 1980s would bring a new set of far-reaching problems to both Hugh Hefner and the Playboy brand.

PART IV
A BRAND IN DECLINE—THE 1980s

TABLE IV **Timeline—The 1980s**

1980: Playboy Channel debuts. Playmate Dorothy Stratten is murdered. Hugh Hefner receives a star on the Hollywood Walk of Fame.

1981: Playboy Enterprises announces the sale of its entire English gaming operations after the British Magistrate revokes the company's gambling license. Playboy is denied a New Jersey gambling license and must accept Elsinore Corporation as a business partner in order for the Playboy Casino to open in Atlantic City.

1982: Christie Hefner is named President of Playboy Enterprises, Inc.

1984: Peter Bogdanovich publishes a book naming Hugh Hefner responsible for Dorothy Stratten's murder. Playboy sells its share of its Atlantic City, New Jersey, casino after 2 years of failed appeals to acquire a gambling license.

1985: U.S. Attorney General forms a federal panel to study pornography; dubbed the Meese Commission. Hugh Hefner suffers a stroke.

1986: Meese Commission accuses 23 major retailers of selling or distributing pornography causing many to stop selling *Playboy* magazine in their stores. Meese Report released. Article in *Newsweek* announces Playboy is about to collapse.

1988: Hefner steps down as Chairman and CEO of Playboy Enterprises, Inc., and names Christie Hefner the new Chairman and CEO. The last Playboy Club closes in Lansing, Michigan.

1989: Hugh Hefner marries Kimberley Conrad and disappears from his role as visible brand champion. The Chicago Playboy Building closes.

CHAPTER 11
A CHANGING WORLD

I think the world and society during the 80s and 90s were kind of at a more conservative time politically, socially and sexually.
  Hugh Hefner, 2003 Interview with the *Hollywood Reporter*

Playboy Enterprises found itself in unfamiliar and uncomfortable territory during the latter half of the 1970s, but problems for the brand would get worse very quickly. The 1980s brought a new focus on conservatism in the macro environment that reached across the United States and affected all parts of the Playboy company. Had the brand not been so strong and so well-recognized around the world, with a loyal base of existing consumers, the 1980s could have been the end of the company.

Trouble plagued Playboy in the 1980s. On the financial front, the magazine was losing market share, the Playboy Clubs were losing money, and the Playboy Casino in London was losing everything. Politically, the government was calling for a heavy-handed crack-down on what it referred to as the threat of pornography, and socially, the emergence of AIDS made people question the Playboy lifestyle overall. In short, there was almost no macro environmental factor that wasn't challenging the Playboy brand throughout the decade.

POLITICS VS. PLAYBOY IN THE 1980s

In 1980, much of the political buzz was about the U.S. Presidential Election held in November of that year. Ronald Reagan's election cleared the way for a conservative movement that was not kind to Playboy or Hugh Hefner, the Playboy brand champion. In fact, much of Reagan's 1980 campaign focused on a need to return to conservative, family values and attacked pornography (among other things) in stark contrast to the conservatism he advocated. His followers became known as the "New Right" reflecting their conservative, or right-leaning, political thinking. Many of his supporters were members of Generation Jones who lived through the optimism of the 1960s led by the Baby Boomer Generation only to find skyrocketing interest and unemployment rates, economic crises, and political instability in the 1970s. In the 1980s, many Americans latched onto a message that harkened back to the conservative and prosperous 1950s. When Ronald Reagan was elected, the country began an immediate shift to a more conservative ideology, and pornography became a target of their attacks. As such, both Playboy and Hugh Hefner were caught in the center of the controversy.

Of course, Hugh Hefner was used to being the target of attacks. From the time *Playboy* magazine debuted in 1953, he had fought against critics and groups that opposed the Playboy lifestyle and the images of nude women found on the pages of the magazine. Hefner responded to attacks in the 1980s the same way he did in the three decades prior—by writing articles in *Playboy* magazine that defended the brand and criticized its attackers. It could be said that the 1980s marked a decade of less turmoil for Americans than they had experienced in the recent past, and therefore, people had more time on their hands to attack things like pornography and label them the causes of the problems in society. However, the messages coming from the political world that denounced pornography gave the conservative movement a loud and broad-reaching voice.

At the same time, the Reagan administration announced a full-scale war on drugs. For years, Hugh Hefner used *Playboy* magazine as a tool to announce his support of marijuana and made it clear that his views about the drug were those of the Playboy brand. After the drug scandal that rocked the brand in the 1970s, Playboy and drugs were tightly linked in people's minds, and that connection was not lost on the politicians behind the war on drugs. In fact, the anti-drug movement of the 1980s and the associated police crackdown on drug use were often linked to the type of lifestyle Playboy advocated. Again, the brand could not escape criticism and controversy at the hands of the U.S. government and politicians looking to gain favor among conservative Americans, many of whom agreed with pointing the finger at Playboy as one of the causes of the problems of society in the 1980s.

SOCIETY VS. PLAYBOY IN THE 1980s

It didn't help Playboy in the 1980s that sexually transmitted diseases were on the rise and divorce rates were up, and despite the availability of contraception devices like the pill, so were illegitimate births. However, the Playboy brand was not prepared for the widespread rise of AIDS that would create a negative backlash throughout the decade against Playboy and the lifestyle the brand promoted, which could not be ignored. In fact, the fear of AIDS that reached a point of hysteria in the 1980s led directly to a decrease in the Playboy Enterprises' bottom line. Suddenly, participating in the sexually liberated lifestyle depicted on the pages of *Playboy* magazine wasn't safe for anyone, and a brand that does not carry a connotation of security is destined for problems.

Furthermore, society followed the influences of the political leaders of the time and shifted to a stronger focus on patriotism, family values, and religion as the ideals to aspire toward. The individual freedoms people rallied for in the previous two decades took a backseat as the economy in the United States prospered and materialism became more the norm than the fantasy. As the world became more global, Americans began to look outside of U.S. borders toward true globalization, and less inwardly at personal freedoms.

While American life wasn't perfect in the 1980s, it moved closer to the 1950s nostalgic ideal than that of the 1960s or 1970s. The Feminist Movement continued, but with less fervor as more women found themselves in higher positions in government and business, and the double-income household became the standard definition of an American family. As divorce rates continued to rise and AIDS spread, people focused more heavily on the importance of marriage and monogamy than on the lifestyle depicted on the pages of *Playboy* magazine. In fact, the Playboy lifestyle became a symbol of irresponsibility. The Baby Boomer Generation was aging, and American values were changing with them. The Playboy brand wasn't positioned to weather the change without taking a beating.

In James R. Patterson's *The Century of Sex: Playboy's History of the Sexual Revolution, 1900–1999*, the author dubs the 1980s as the time of "The Great Repression." However, despite the conservative movement, sex became more mainstream in the United States than ever with cable television programming, movies, and books pushing the envelope of accepted decency. As sex experts such as Dr. Ruth Westheimer grew in celebrity, the decade struggled between "the great repression" and a "great permission" that had grown during the previous decade (p. 378). American consumers struggled between the accessibility of sex and the conservative movement, and of course, the struggle brought familiar controversy to Playboy and Hugh Hefner.

However, unlike the response Hefner and Playboy received to messages of sexual freedom and individual liberties in the three prior decades, the 1980s found the Playboy brand with a bigger target on its back from politicians and activists looking for a place to lay blame more so than ever. Simply retaliating with articles in *Playboy* magazine wouldn't be enough to defend the brand in the 1980s. Instead, the decade would force another restructuring of the Playboy company, and brand extensions would become more focused. Decades of unprecedented growth came to an end and things had to change for the brand to survive.

THE LONGEVITY OF THE PLAYBOY BRAND

The Playboy brand had reached its maturity level in the 1970s and was already on its decline when the 1980s began. It's the lifecycle all brands follow. The goal of the company behind a brand on decline is to find new ways to breathe life into that brand and keep it alive. Inevitably, increased competition, a changing macro environment, and a shift in consumer tastes will force a brand that has not planned far enough into the future into decline. In the 1980s, Playboy became one of those brands that was forced into decline with no plan in place to extend its lifecycle (see Box 11.1 for more examples of brands in decline).

Companies can use a variety of tactics to lengthen a brand's lifecycle. Each requires constant monitoring and analysis of the brand's position within the marketplace and against competitors, influences on the market environment related to new technology, consumer preferences, and so on. For example, companies can

- *Introduce line extensions*: Conduct ongoing research to uncover opportunities for extending the brand into new products within the existing market. Coca-Cola is an example of a brand that thrives on line extensions such as Coca-Cola, Diet Coke, Caffeine Free Coke, Diet Coke with Lemon, Coca-Cola Zero, and so on.

- *Expand into new markets*: Find new markets to expand the brand's reach, including globalization. For example, the Disney Company has expanded its theme park brand into a number of countries outside of the United States such as China (Hong Kong), Japan (Tokyo), and France (Paris).
- *Introduce category extensions*: Find new categories where the brand name could work on a new or existing (rebranded) product. Health and beauty consumer products use this tactic frequently. For example, Unilever's Dove began as a bar soap. Today, you can find the Dove brand name on hand soap, bath gel, shampoo, hair conditioners, hair styling products, and more.
- Create new uses for existing products under the brand umbrella: Create new ways consumers can use existing products. For example, mobile phones began as just phones. Today, with products like the iPhone from Apple, consumers can use their mobile phones as cameras and calculators, for text messaging, email, Internet browsing, playing games, and more.

BOX 11.1 Brands that faced decline and survived with mixed results

Harley Davidson, Polaroid, Apple, Microsoft—these are just a few examples of well-known brands that have found themselves in decline. For Harley Davidson, decline came in the 1970s from inexpensive Japanese competitor motorcycles that stole market share. To compete, Harley Davidson made the mistake of introducing its own less expensive motorcycles. The move confused loyal Harley Davidson consumers who expected high quality from the brand. The Harley Davidson brand and sales suffered, and in the end, the company made significant investments to regain its position as the high-quality, innovative engineering brand. Today, Harley Davidson remains one of the strongest cult brands in history.

The story for Polaroid was a bit different. Polaroid's decline came because the company became complacent and failed to recognize the changing macro environment. Technological advances in the 1990s took a toll on Polaroid which had dominated the instant photography category for years. When digital cameras hit the marketplace and quickly became the standard, Polaroid scrambled to catch up. The Polaroid brand managed to survive, but not without the

> company going bankrupt. Today, Polaroid owns a small market share as brands such as Canon and Nikon dominate the digital photography market.
>
> Another example of a brand in decline was The Gap who realized in the 1990s that its target market was getting older, and the younger demographic was far more attractive in terms of driving short-term revenues. As such, The Gap all but turned its back on its loyal customer audience when it released a series of marketing campaigns clearly targeted to teenagers and young adults. The Gap's core customer base was ignored, and the customers responded by taking their business elsewhere.

Each strategy listed above requires long-term strategic planning *before* the brand reaches maturity in order to be most effective. In the 1980s, the Playboy brand was already past maturity and in decline. The strategies typically employed to extend a brand's lifecycle were not in place. Rapid overexpansion of the brand in the three prior decades left the brand without the resources and expertise needed to maintain them all, and something had to give. In addition, growing competition from other magazines and television left Playboy without a strong message of differentiation. Instead, a series of conflicting positions, brand messages, and disjointed brand extensions further confused consumers.

In short, the macro environment dominated much of the Playboy brand decline in the 1970s and 1980s. Changing consumer interests, increased communication and distribution points, and new competitors (many of which were low-cost competitors who could move much more quickly than Playboy could or would) challenged Playboy from all sides, but Playboy failed to keep tabs on the changing macro environment and make the necessary investments to proactively address those changes from the inside. It could be said that much of Playboy's problems came from failed management that became too comfortable with the success of the Playboy brand and allowed it to spiral out of control before it would inevitably come crashing down.

It could also be argued that the Playboy brand survived the macro environment of the 1980s because it was the pioneer brand with extraordinary value. It is commonly accepted among marketing experts that it's better to be first to market (the pioneer brand) than it is to be best (the challenging brand), because the pioneer brand has the opportunity to own a word in consumers' minds before competitors can challenge it and dilute the power of that brand association. Playboy definitely benefited from being the pioneer brand during the 1980s. Without the brand equity that Playboy had developed since its debut in 1953, its story may have been different (see Box 11.2 for more

> **BOX 11.2 Brand survival stories**
>
> There are a number of brands that survived decline thanks to the valuable brand equity that they held. Perhaps one of the most interesting examples is Martha Stewart who had spent years building her brand through a variety of targeted extensions such as television shows, books, a magazine, a Web site, products for the home such as bed linens, kitchen and bath products, and more. At the peak of her brand's success, Stewart was found guilty of violating insider trading laws and was sentenced to spend several months in prison. Many people believed the ruling would be the end of Martha Stewart's career, her company, and her brand. However, the Martha Stewart brand had enormous equity. Consumers still believed in the brand's consistent promise, and the majority of them were able to disassociate Stewart's financial problems from her brand. In the end, Martha Stewart, her company, and her brand prevailed, and today, they continue to grow and thrive.
>
> Another example of a brand that survived thanks to its inherent equity is the Volkswagen Beetle. The "Bug" debuted in 1938, and it became an iconic car both for its design and its appearance in popular culture throughout the 1960s and into the 1970s. However, it grew outdated and old-fashioned for U.S. consumers as the 1970s progressed. Volkswagen shifted focus from the Beetle to other models such as the Volkswagen Golf, and the Beetle became a brand that had lost its position and its popularity. No one could have expected that Volkswagen would release the New Beetle in 1998. Drawing on the brand equity that the Volkswagen Beetle still held, the nostalgia of older consumers who remembered riding in earlier models of the Beetle in their youths, and injecting a modern design, the New Beetle drew immediate attention. Volkswagen produced a small number of New Beetles initially to create a perceived shortage and paired that strategy with creative online and offline marketing campaigns. The New Beetle was an instant success and represented how brand equity can survive even after that brand all but disappears.

examples of brands that survived thanks to their existing equity). However, the Playboy brand was already deeply rooted in American culture by the 1980s. It was already a strong cult brand with an audience of core consumers who felt deeply loyal to it. The losses that Playboy Enterprises experienced in the 1980s were the result of explosive growth in the decades prior that almost no brand or company could sustain for long.

The fact that Playboy did grow so far, so fast is a testament to the Playboy product following the fundamental business truth discussed throughout this book: it's far easier to create a product to meet consumers' existing needs than it is to create a perceived need to meet the business goals of an existing product. Second, it's an example of the power of a strong brand champion, Hugh Hefner, playing the role of visible brand-advocate since the brand's inception. The amazing part of the story is not only that Playboy survived the decade but did so with renewed hope for the future. Much of Playboy's reformation in the 1980s came from its new CEO, Christie Hefner, and a new focus on what the Playboy brand was originally meant to represent when it was first launched. A renewed focus in the 1980s would breathe new life into the brand in the 1990s and 2000s that no one could have anticipated.

CHAPTER 12

A CHANGING OF THE GUARD

I didn't join Playboy thinking I'd stay.
Christie Hefner, 2003 Interview
with Charlie Rose

In the 1970s, the Playboy Casinos in England were booming. While other parts of Playboy Enterprises were struggling, Playboy Clubs were closing, *Playboy* magazine sales were falling, and the future looked bleak, the company placed much of its fate on the success of its casinos. In essence, the company made the same mistake it had made time and time again—focusing on short-term gains rather than long-term, sustainable strategies. In 1979, trouble began for Playboy's English gaming operations when the British Gaming Board began investigating the British casinos for illegal activities, specifically, proof that a U.S. company, Playboy Enterprises, was controlling the British casinos in violation of the British Gaming Act.

By 1980, the *Wall Street Journal* reported that Playboy Enterprises' English casinos accounted for 85% of the company's earnings. When the British Magistrate reviewed the evidence compiled during investigations into the operations of the English Playboy casinos, he ruled against Playboy Enterprises, and the company lost its British gaming license in October 1981. The blow to the company was nearly catastrophic. The company had placed all its hopes of survival on its British casinos and had lost 85% of its income with a single ruling. There would be no rebound, and Playboy Enterprises was forced to sell its entire English gambling operation in November 1981 for a mere $31.4 million—one-tenth of its value.

A BRAND IN DECLINE—THE 1980s

Playboy Enterprises lost most of its earnings when it was forced to sell its casinos in England, and the company found itself in a place of desperation. Unfortunately, business on its home turf wasn't going much better. In 1979, Playboy Enterprises began construction on an enormous casino in Atlantic City, New Jersey, hoping to achieve the same kind of success it had been experiencing overseas at the time. The casino cost $135 million to build over the course of 2 years. According to *Business Week*, Playboy Enterprises invested half of the company's total equity into the project but felt justified in the investment believing it would deliver over $30 million per year in profits (after taxes). Most outsiders viewed the investment as highly risky. Americans were facing a weak economy and were greatly affected by the oil crisis of 1979. The Atlantic City gaming market was already highly competitive, and Playboy's foray into gaming there was viewed negatively long before news got out of the company's troubles with its English gaming operations. However, Playboy Enterprises saw dollar signs from its successful English operations and pushed forward with the Atlantic City project in 1979.

As ground broke in Atlantic City, news broke of the investigation into illegal activities in Playboy's English gaming operations. Playboy's problems would grow exponentially as the opening date of the Atlantic City casino moved closer. Unable to secure financing and a gambling license for the Atlantic City casino due to the company's problems with the British Playboy casinos, Playboy Enterprises was forced to take on a business partner, Elsinore Corporation. By allowing Elsinore Corporation to run the operation, the companies were able to obtain a temporary gaming license.

The doors to the new casino on the New Jersey shore opened in April 1981 with the Playboy logo prominently displayed atop the 22-story building and Playboy bunnies working the casino floor, but things would deteriorate very quickly. When the British Magistrate denied Playboy's British gambling license in October 1981, the Division of Gambling in New Jersey took notice. In November 1981, Playboy's request for a permanent gambling license in Atlantic City was denied.

Unlike the quick sale of its British gaming operations, Playboy Enterprises was prepared to fight the denial of its Atlantic City gambling license. With a $135 investment on the line, the company simply couldn't afford to walk away without a fight. However, after 2 years of appeals, Playboy cut its losses and sold its 45.7% interest in the casino to Elsinore Corporation in April 1984. By June of the same year, all vestiges of Playboy, including the Playboy sign, were removed from the casino. With all areas of its business doing poorly, Playboy Enterprises had reached rock bottom, or so it thought.

THE MEESE REPORT ATTACKS PLAYBOY

On May 20, 1985, U.S. Attorney General Edwin Meese announced he would lead an investigation ordered by President Ronald Reagan into pornography, particularly the link between pornography and sexual crimes. Meese and his panel would come to be known as the Meese Commission. The group targeted *Playboy, Penthouse,* and *Hustler* as root causes of rape, child molestation, and violent crime in a 1,960-page report published in July 1986 (dubbed the Meese Report). The problems for Playboy didn't come so much from the content of the final report, which was attacked from people of all walks of life for its bias, but from the entire investigative process.

Throughout the course of the federally funded, year-long Meese Commission investigation, Playboy and Hugh Hefner were continually attacked, which would inevitably tarnish the brand over time. Blame for society's problems was squarely placed on the shoulders of Hugh Hefner and the Playboy lifestyle he advocated. During the investigation, Hefner was compared to Hitler and the content of Playboy to Nazi literature. This wasn't the first time such an analogy was made. A decade earlier, Gloria Steinem made a similar comparison in an article she published in *McCall's* magazine (discussed in more detail in Chapter 8). In the final Meese Report, pornography was compared to Communism, "That the Communist Party is a lawful organization does not prevent most Americans from finding its tenets abhorrent, and the same holds true for a wide variety of sexually-oriented material." This was not the kind of publicity Playboy needed in the 1980s.

From June 1985 to January 1986, the Meese Commission held a series of highly publicized public hearings in an attempt to link pornography to violence and the ills of society. During that time, brand names like Playboy were continually mentioned and criticized. The court of public opinion ruled against Playboy during the Meese Commission's investigation. In early 1986, the Meese Commission began to target not just the makers of pornography but also the distributors when it sent letters to 23 retailers, including companies like Coca-Cola, Time, Inc., CBS, Simon & Schuster, Vogue, Southland Corporation (owner of 7–11), and more, warning them that the commission planned to publish a list of distributors of pornography. The letters told those companies that not responding equated to acquiescence. Many of the companies on the list responded to the Meese Commission's threats and dropped *Playboy* and similar materials from their store shelves. By mid-1986, Southland Corporation, Rite Aid Drug Stores, Dart Drug Corporation, Stop-N-Go, Lawson's Milk Company, and J.C. Penney stopped selling Playboy merchandise.

Playboy Enterprises, along with the American Booksellers Association and the Council for Periodical Distributors Association, filed a lawsuit in 1986 claiming the Meese Commission was creating a blacklist that coerced companies into refusing to sell products which had not been ruled obscene by a court of law. In July 1986, a federal district court judge ruled that the letters were both coercive and threatening and forced the Meese Commission to retract them; however, the damage had been done. The number of *Playboy* magazine and merchandise distributors did not fully rebound, and the brand name had been irreparably harmed.

Ultimately, the Meese Report was released the same month and became the center of its own publicity mine field as people questioned its purpose and its findings. While the final report found no specific links between pornography and violence, the Playboy brand had been sufficiently trounced. After the collapse of Playboy's gaming operations 2 years earlier, many thought the brand was beyond repair in 1986. In fact, a cover story in *Newsweek* in August 1986 announced that Playboy Enterprises was on the verge of collapse.

CHRISTIE HEFNER TAKES CONTROL

While the 1980s were wrought with problems for Playboy Enterprises, there was a breath of fresh air waiting in the wings. Christie Hefner graduated from Brandeis College summa cum laude and joined Playboy Enterprises in 1975. While she had plans to become a lawyer, her father suggested she give the business world a try in the hopes she would become heir apparent to his legacy. Christie joined Playboy Enterprises as special assistant to her father and as such gained exposure to many areas of the company very quickly. Her first big role came soon after she started at Playboy Enterprises when she became operator of Playtique, the boutique inside the Playboy Building in Chicago, an experience she cites as giving her the savvy into running a business. She managed public relations for the year-long celebration of the 25th anniversary of *Playboy* magazine and chaired the New

Publications Group, where she and a team evaluated new magazine opportunities.

In 1978, Derick Daniels was named the new president of Playboy Enterprises during the corporate reorganization that began in 1976 after Playboy Enterprises realized it was losing money with little chance of reversal. When Daniels came on board, he understood part of his role would be to mentor Christie Hefner. By 1978, she rose to Corporate Vice President and Publisher of two Playboy consumer guides. During her quick rise through the ranks of Playboy Enterprises, she was viewed in stark contrast to her father. While Hugh Hefner made no secret of his disinterest in business, Christie Hefner displayed keen business ability. Her business intelligence wasn't the only thing that Playboy Enterprises liked about her. She was also a woman, which meant she tempered many of the anti-feminist attacks against the Playboy brand. Christie was well-liked, intelligent, and carried the Hefner name. Her presence in Playboy Enterprises brought renewed hope.

In 1982, Hugh Hefner named his daughter President of Playboy Enterprises. The 29-year old took the reins of a company that was losing money following the closure of the British gaming operations, the debacle at the Atlantic City casino, lower sales of *Playboy* magazine, and years of clubs and hotels operating in the red. It was a time when many people thought the young president could not have a measurable impact on the company and turnaround was unlikely. However, Christie Hefner immediately made her business prowess known and made a commitment to refocus the company by concentrating on the brand's strengths.

In simplest terms, Christie Hefner did exactly what needed to be done years prior and refocused the brand that had over-expanded too quickly. The time was overdue for the brand to contract, but the hope of Christie Hefner and Playboy Enterprises was that it wasn't too late. Of course, the company's first priority was short-term solvency. To achieve that goal, Christie Hefner divested the company of its most unprofitable projects in order to reallocate resources and focus on the company's core businesses. She sold Playboy Books within her first few months of tenure as president and began closing more Playboy Clubs. By the mid-1980s, most of the Playboy Clubs were closed, including those in Chicago, New York, and Los Angeles. Consumers had shown that experiencing the Playboy brand in clubs was no longer of interest. Consumer preferences had changed, and Playboy was slow to recognize the shift. However, by 1988, the last Playboy Club closed in Lansing, Michigan.

A BRAND IN DECLINE—THE 1980s

After Christie Hefner took on her role as president of Playboy Enterprises, the company's strategy moved from trying to be a brand with a wide focus to one with a narrow focus. Hefner believed the company's strength was as a communications company, and all brand activity should support that core competency. A narrow focus would allow the brand to dominate its core markets and grow through measured strategies rather than the short-sighted approach used in previous decades. The world had changed, and it was time for the Playboy brand to change in order to keep up.

Christie Hefner recognized television as the next medium the Playboy brand could conquer by providing Playboy customers with a new way to experience the brand. The strategy made sense for an inclusive relationship brand like Playboy that relied heavily on providing a variety of ways that consumers could self-select how they wanted to interact with and experience the brand. With the debut of the Playboy Channel in 1980 (discussed in detail in Chapter 13), much effort would go into developing a television strategy for the Playboy brand over the course of the decade. Playboy's foray into television would not proceed without obstacles, particularly from religious groups who pressured cable companies to drop the Playboy Channel from their channel lineup offerings. However, Hefner and Playboy Enterprises continued to pursue a television presence for the Playboy brand despite the challenges.

At the same time, increased attention was placed on *Playboy* magazine. The flagship product for the brand was still the number one men's magazine in the world, despite circulation falling to less than 4 million copies per month by the mid-1980s. Playboy Enterprises refocused on the brand's strength from the magazine and looked for ways to leverage that brand equity to rebuild the company. In 1986, the Playboy Enterprises Annual Report stated that the company had lost $62 million, and *Playboy* magazine became the symbol of hope for the future. The magazine was smaller than it had been a decade earlier, but it was still profitable. The goal in the mid-1980s was to find ways to make the magazine and the Playboy brand relevant again. The key to success became finding ways to rebuild the brand after the damage that had been done to it in the prior years.

When the 1980s began, *Playboy* magazine had been struggling with redefining its role within the men's magazine market. Competitive attacks from hard-core pornographic publications such as *Penthouse* and *Hustler* in the 1970s had caused Playboy to pursue a reactionary strategy, and rather than leading the industry as the pioneer brand,

Playboy changed its strategy to compete with the brand challengers. The strategy backfired, all differentiation was lost, and Playboy consumers were confused. The new focus on the magazine in the 1980s meant the content needed to be revamped to differentiate the brand from competitors, but customer expectations for the brand still needed to be met. The right balance had to be found between pornography and content in order to reposition *Playboy* as a general interest men's magazine.

Much of the features found on the pages of *Playboy* in the early 1980s would remain the same such as interviews, stories, pop culture articles, and articles written from a strong liberal point of view advocating personal freedoms. However, in order to keep the magazine relevant to a new generation of consumers, *Playboy* was revamped in the middle of the decade. Readers found fewer political articles and more service and lifestyle pieces, akin to the format of the original *Playboy* magazine of the 1950s. Articles focused on cooking, clothes, decorating, and so on to appeal to the changing male demographic that was now made up of a growing number of divorced men and men who chose to get married later in life. The magazine sought to appeal to a new audience of 20- and 30-something, young urban professionals—the "yuppies" of the 1980s. This audience was characterized by a stronger interest in materialism than politics. They were financially secure, often put off getting married and having children until later in life, and they were interested in further economic advancement. The audience was a natural match for the newly revamped *Playboy* magazine.

Concurrently, steps were taken to make the magazine appear to be of a higher quality than those published by competitors. A new staple-less format was introduced to give the magazine a high-end look, and more articles were printed that talked about business, finance, success, and Corporate America. Images and articles about businessmen *and* businesswomen could now be found on the pages of *Playboy.* Under Christie Hefner's guidance, *Playboy* repositioned as a publication that advocated marriage, relationships, and love as being able to coexist with work and sex. The magazine focused on men and women living together, working together, loving together, and playing together. The Playboy brand became an inclusive relationship brand again, and consumers responded positively to the change (see Box 12.1 for other examples of brands that have been repositioned successfully).

In September 1988, Hugh Hefner removed himself completely from the day-to-day business operations of the company he started 43 years

A BRAND IN DECLINE—THE 1980s

> **BOX 12.1** The repositioning of Clorox and Hyundai
>
> Clorox has always been linked to bleach. Whether a customer needs to bleach her clothes or her kitchen floor, Clorox is one of the first (and possibly the only) brands people think of. Clorox owns the word bleach in consumers' minds. It's the pioneer brand and dominates its market. However, when consumers began to become more environmentally conscious and began searching for products that did not use harsh chemicals (including bleach alternatives), Clorox began to feel the pinch in sales. Today, Clorox continues to try to retain market share despite the "chemical-free" trend. Brand extensions such as Clorox products specifically intended for "harsh" jobs, including floor and toilet bowl cleaning, were launched as was a line of eco-friendly cleaning products called Clorox Green Works. However, Clorox still needed to find a way to ensure its core bleach product survived despite changing consumer preferences for gentler cleaning products (similar to how Playboy Enterprises has struggled to find ways to ensure its core magazine product survived).
>
> For years, Clorox has been continuing its push to reposition its product as less harsh than people have always thought. An ad campaign launched in January 2009 used television commercials to show consumers that Clorox can safely be used to sanitize household items, even baby items such as bottles and toys. Clorox faces an uphill battle in converting consumers in large numbers to give up their perceptions of the brand as a harsh chemical. However, the effort continues.
>
> Another example of a company that has pursued brand repositioning is Hyundai. In the early days of the Hyundai brand, it owned the word "cheap" in consumers' minds. In order to reposition the brand, the company redesigned its cars to be more contemporary and launched an unprecedented warranty program (10 years or 100,000 miles) that competitors are still trying to copy. Consumer perceptions were changed as the new car styling attracted their eyes and the warranty appealed to their sense of trust and security. It was a genius marketing effort that worked.

earlier and named Christie Hefner Chairman and CEO of Playboy Enterprises, Inc, while he remained involved in major strategic decisions. A year later, Christie Hefner moved Playboy Enterprises from the massive building it occupied in Chicago to a smaller office space, saving the company millions of dollars each year. Under her leadership, the company tried to reposition the Playboy brand to appeal to a broader, mainstream audience with a new brand message of, "Quality fun for grown-ups" (Watts, p. 423).

Christie Hefner believed that the new audience for a repositioned Playboy brand could be as high as 40 million. Steps had been taken to rebuild the brand as the leader of its core markets and refocus on its most profitable segments, and a brand that could have disappeared in the 1980s emerged at the end of the decade with a good chance for survival. The next decade would find the brand and the Playboy Enterprises' stock price on a relatively stable growth track.

CHAPTER 13
A CHANGE OF COURSE

I'm not as driven as I used to be. Part of that was the ability to pass off some of the business end to my daughter and focus on the part of the Playboy company that I really cared about, which is the magazine and the creative end of it.
Hugh Hefner, *80* by Gerald Gardner and Jim Bellows

While Playboy Enterprises was plagued with financial, political, and social challenges throughout the 1980s, Hugh Hefner, as the brand champion, was always targeted at the heart of the controversies around the brand. A new conservative movement marked the political, religious, and social views of the decade, and Hugh Hefner and the Playboy brand's public links to sexual liberation and drugs were the topic of choice for many Americans. The cloud hanging over the Playboy brand would get darker before it would clear.

CONTROVERSY TAKES A TOLL ON THE BRAND CHAMPION

On August 15, 1980, Playmate Dorothy Stratten was murdered by her estranged husband, Paul Snider (upon learning of her affair with film director Peter Bogdanovich) who then turned his gun on himself and committed suicide. The event ushered in a decade of problems for Hugh Hefner and Playboy. The death of Dorothy Stratten was tragic and gave the media an opportunity to link Hefner and Playboy directly with violence and deviant behavior. On November 5, 1980, *Village Voice* writer Teresa Carpenter wrote a scathing article that blamed Stratten's death on three men saying, "Dorothy Stratten was the focus of the dreams and ambitions of three men. One killed her." According to Carpenter, "Dorothy Stratten was less memorable for herself than for the yearnings she evoked: in Snider a lust for the score; in Hefner a longing for a star; in Bogdanovich a desire for the eternal ingénue. She was a catalyst for a cycle of ambitions which revealed its players less wicked, perhaps, than pathetic" (p. 12).

Carpenter wrote that Hefner used Stratten in order to obtain legitimacy in Hollywood by pushing her into a career in movies and giving him the opportunity to say that Playboy had created a star. Carpenter's article was republished in various publications and was referenced throughout the media. Later, Carpenter won the 1981 Pulitzer Prize for feature writing for the article. The finger had been pointed squarely at Hugh Hefner and Playboy, and the media frenzy that followed was not what the Playboy brand needed in the early 1980s.

In his defense, Hugh Hefner responded to Carpenter's attack with his own article in *Playboy* magazine. Hefner defended Stratten and Playboy in his article, and the public formed its own opinions about the connection between Playboy and Stratten's death. However, the damage to the brand had been done and simply added fuel to the conservative movement against pornography, violence, and Playboy that would follow with the election of President Ronald Reagan in 1980 and the formation of the Meese Commission in 1985. When Peter Bogdanovich published his own book about Stratten's murder, *The Killing of the Unicorn: Dorothy Stratten, 1960–1980*, he named Hefner as the man responsible for her death. Hefner was consumed with preserving his reputation in the former half of the 1980s. Ultimately, Bogdanovich apologized for blaming Stratten's murder on Hefner, but again, the damage had already been done to Hefner and the Playboy brand.

As Hugh Hefner navigated unfriendly fire from the press following Dorothy Stratten's murder, he was also faced with a company that was close to losing 85% of its earnings as the British Magistrate investigated Playboy's British gaming license. He had spent his recent past extricating himself more and more from the business operations of Playboy Enterprises and it showed in January 1982 when he testified in a hearing with the New Jersey Casino Control Commission following the November 1981 denial by the Division of Gaming Enforcement of Playboy Enterprises' request for a gaming license in Atlantic City. The brand champion failed miserably, providing testimony that proved he had not prepared for the important event. He couldn't remember key facts and had obviously not read the report into the investigation by the Division of Gaming Enforcement prior to the trial. In the end, his absence from his company had a direct and significant negative impact on Playboy Enterprises. By 1984, Playboy Enterprises abandoned its appeals of the rejected gaming license and sold its 47.5% share in the Atlantic City Playboy Casino. The $135 million project was a complete loss both financially and in terms of its impact on the Playboy brand.

Hugh Hefner had made it clear for many years that the business side of Playboy did not appeal to him. He enjoyed playing his role of brand champion, working to preserve personal freedoms, protecting the First Amendment (see Box 13.1 for a list of awards Hefner received in the 1980s), and watching his celebrity grow, but he was not interested in the daily operations of a company. Throughout the previous three decades, business analysts repeatedly attacked Hefner for his lack of business skills, directly linking his inabilities to lead his organization

---

BOX 13.1   Awards and honors bestowed upon Hugh Hefner during the 1980s

(Adapted from PlayboyEnterprises.com)

- **1980**: Hugh Hefner receives the First Amendment Freedom Award of the B'nai B'rith Anti-Defamation League of Los Angeles for his efforts to protect individual freedom.
- **1980**: Hugh Hefner receives a star on the Hollywood Walk of Fame.
- **1983**: Chicago Mayor Harold Washington declares Hugh M. Hefner Day to recognize Hefner's contributions to the business world.
- **1984**: Mayor Tom Bradley of Los Angeles presents Hugh Hefner with a commendation for his cultural contributions to the city such as the Playboy Jazz Festival.
- **1987**: Hugh Hefner receives the Southern California Cable Association Award for his ongoing efforts to defend the First Amendment.
- **1989**: Hugh Hefner is inducted into *Folio* magazine's Publishing Hall of Fame.

A CHANGE OF COURSE

to the decline in business for the company. Analysts accused Hefner of investing in projects that suited his personal interests on a whim with no research or strategy. When *Newsweek* ran an article in August 1986 stating that Playboy was nearing collapse, Hugh Hefner's picture donned the cover. Critics attacked the Playboy brand as irrelevant and Hefner's parties and lifestyle as boring by the standards of consumers in the 1980s. They called Playboy a brand that was fixated on the rebellious decades of the 1960s and 1970s which failed to recognize that the world around it, and the people within that world, had changed. In many ways, they were right.

Hefner did not go down without a fight. He focused his efforts in the 1980s on preserving his reputation and the brand he had spent most of his life building. However, his fight and his lifestyle took a toll on his health, and in 1985, the Playboy brand champion suffered a stroke that would remove him from the spotlight completely for several weeks. In interviews after his stroke, Hefner has repeatedly referred to it as a "stroke of luck," claiming it caused him to refocus his life. He reinvented himself for the fourth time in as many decades. Hefner stopped smoking and pursued a healthier lifestyle. In 1988, he made the decision to step down from his role as the leader of Playboy Enterprises and named his daughter, Christie Hefner, Chairman and CEO.

A TURN TO MERCHANDISING

Christie Hefner had already proven herself capable of leading Playboy Enterprises. Since she became president in 1982, she had taken steps to consolidate the Playboy Enterprises business operations and reintroduce the company as a leading communications organization. She spearheaded changes that touched all facets of the company and restructured a company that was nearing collapse in 1986 to showing signs of survival and a possible rebirth by the latter part of the decade. The primary focus, however, was on rebuilding the equity of the Playboy brand, the company's strongest asset. As the company stripped itself to its core and divested business endeavors that were draining resources and money, the strength of the Playboy brand rose to the top.

Suddenly, merchandising the Playboy brand became the most profitable segment of Playboy Enterprises. Despite the many challenges the brand had faced in its nearly 50-year lifecycle, it still held enormous value. With the growth of its merchandising business, the company learned that the Playboy brand appealed to consumers in multiple market segments and various demographic groups. Women, men, young, and old consumers were attracted to the Playboy brand and bought products emblazoned with the bunny logo on them. Licensing the Playboy brand name and iconic Bunny logo was a lucrative venture. Consumers typically purchase branded merchandise in patterns that match the changing economy, so licensing originally brought Playboy inconsistent earnings. However, the profit margin for Playboy's licensing business was very high. It's an area that Christie Hefner recognized as being capable of carrying the company in the long term (see Box 13.2 for more stories of brand merchandising success).

> **BOX 13.2 Success stories of extending and merchandising brands**
>
> In 1888, the National Geographic Society was created and 9 months later, the first issue of *National Geographic* magazine was published. Over the next century, the National Geographic brand name would extend to television specials and eventually its own cable television network, additional magazines, books, merchandise (through the National Geographic catalog), maps, photography, and more. Today, consumers can experience the National Geographic brand in a variety of ways and purchase a myriad of products with the National Geographic brand association. That brand connection creates a perception of quality and trust thanks to the incredible brand equity of National Geographic, which is known and recognized around the world.
>
> The entertainment world also provides a plethora of examples of merchandising success stories. Brands such as Star Wars, Star Trek, and Disney have earned billions of dollars and sustained their lifecycles indefinitely through merchandising. Even comic book characters such as Spider-Man and Batman have evolved and grown through merchandising. Celebrities, themselves, have used merchandising to extend their careers, realizing the income potential licensing their names can deliver. In the 2000s, it's common for male and female celebrities to license their names to appear on clothing, perfumes, and more. For example, in the 2000s alone, Mariah Carey, Sarah Jessica Parker, Britney Spears, Jessica Simpson, Paris Hilton, Gwen

> Stefani, Jennifer Lopez, Christina Aguilera, Kate Moss, Kylie Minogue, Celine Dion, Hillary Duff, Victoria (and David) Beckham, Tim McGraw, Sean Combs, Derek Jeter, and Usher have all licensed their names to appear on perfume and cologne bottles. That's just a sample from the list of celebrities who have jumped on the brand name licensing bandwagon and reaped the financial rewards.
>
> Similarly, consumer product brands such as Coca-Cola, Harley Davidson, and Budweiser have increased their companies' bottom lines through merchandising. It's not unusual to see a Coca-Cola, Harley Davidson, or Budweiser calendar, T-shirt, and so on. Brands with equity can make a lot of money through merchandising, and more companies realize that everyday. That's why many strange brand extensions make it to market (think of Donald Trump Steaks and Precious Moments Coffins, both launched in 2007). The key is for companies to pursue merchandise and licensing opportunities that consistently communicate the brand's promise rather than confusing customers and failing to meet their expectations for the brand.

The process to ramp up Playboy's licensing business in the 1980s started slowly and used a more focused approach than had been followed in the past. Effort was made to choose opportunities to put the Playboy brand name and logo on the products that were of high quality and accurately represented the brand. The company pursued joint ventures with business partners that offered experience and distribution points which Playboy Enterprises did not have as well as licenses with royalty payments attached to them. Playboy Enterprises also repackaged existing photos, articles, and interviews for use in new products (e.g., reselling Playboy photos or repurposing them in Playboy calendars). By the end of the decade, Playboy had approximately 60 product licenses around the world, and the brand could be seen on a growing list of items found in a wide variety of outlets.

Ongoing success and continued growth for Playboy Enterprises would focus on a continued brand contraction strategy that focused on the company's primary areas of expertise, media and communications, as well as on highly focused new brand extensions. However, merchandising steadily became a growing piece of that strategy as other parts of the Playboy empire struggled. The equity that had been built in the Playboy brand over the course of the previous three decades was strong. In a 1992 *Folio* magazine article by Reed Phillips, the then Playboy senior vice president of circulation and planning, he had said that the Playboy brand was "the second most recognized trade symbol in the world (after Coca-Cola's red and white wave)." In the 1980s, Playboy's licensing business experienced a 54% profit margin in comparison to a successful magazine's expected 10% to 15% profit margin. Playboy Enterprises, led by Christie Hefner, made the wise decision to invest in growing its licensing business, and that decision would pay off in years to come.

MOVING INTO TELEVISION

Christie Hefner recognized the importance of leveraging the television market as a new way for consumers to experience the Playboy brand. In the 1980s, cable television presented a new opportunity for Playboy Enterprises to create a branded network with original programming that would help achieve those goals. During a time when cable television was in its infancy, Playboy Enterprises fought for space within the small 35–40 channel lineups cable operators carried. When addressable cable boxes entered the picture, Playboy found a new opportunity to offer its content as a premium service alongside of other branded networks such as the Disney Channel.

Playboy's foray into bringing its valuable brand to television showed the company's leaders that the Playboy consumer audience could be divided into two main audiences—loyal cult brand followers and occasional, impulse buyers. It was this audience of impulse buyers that helped make Playboy's television efforts successful from the beginning. As pay-per-view cable television grew in the latter part of the decade, consumers showed that they were willing to pay for Playboy content—both loyal consumers who paid for Playboy channel subscriptions and impulse buyers who bought chunks of time. In fact, Playboy was the first company to offer pay-per-view content piecemeal, and it worked. Consumers consistently purchased Playboy content in blocks of time, particularly on Friday and Saturday nights, supporting the company's strategy of offering Playboy Weekends to consumers who weren't interested in purchasing 24-hours access.

The strategy would drive earnings into the next decade, and as usual, Playboy Enterprises would enjoy that short-term success but neglect to plan beyond its current success. Technology and consumer preferences were changing rapidly. The move from analog cable television

A CHANGE OF COURSE

to digital cable and a pay-per-view business model happened very fast. Playboy enjoyed the profits pay-per-view delivered, but lacked the foresight to plan for the next phase of technological advancements for television viewing and consumption.

While Playboy Enterprises' investment into television wasn't cheap, Christie Hefner believed it would pay off in time (see Box 13.3 to learn about Hallmark's venture in television). By delivering original, branded content with the quality Playboy was known for, the company returned to its roots as a relationship brand that provided multiple ways for consumers to experience the brand but in a more appropriate mix for the 1980s audience. The goal was to find new ways for consumers to make personal connections with the Playboy brand, and Hefner and the Playboy leadership team placed their bets on two strategies: television and growing its publishing business internationally.

However, Playboy Enterprises would struggle with finding the right recipe for success for many years. First, the company was entering new

---

BOX 13.3   The Hallmark Channel

Very few brands have made a successful transition from one media or business into creating their own television networks. Other brands have had varying successes teaming up with established networks, but the investment required to start a network from scratch is significant and the risks are even greater. Hallmark found some success when it launched the branded Hallmark Channel (and its sister station, the Hallmark Movie Channel) in 2001. The network is owned by NBC Universal in all countries but the United States, where it is owned by Crown Media (a public company, but Hallmark Entertainment, LLC owns enough stock to control 91% of voting power), who licenses the Hallmark brand name. The network airs family-friendly programs and movies.

Today, the Hallmark Channel is available in over 100 countries. Its audience share is small, but the licensing fees are significant for Hallmark. For NBC Universal and Crown Media, the Hallmark brand name brings recognition, a positive perception of quality, and an association to family values in consumers' minds. In 2008, Crown Media reported record ratings, expanded distribution, and increased earnings from the Hallmark Channel, citing the power of its programming and the Hallmark brand as key contributors to the network's growth.

businesses where it lacked experience and expertise. Second, competition and the availability of sexually explicit content became more prevalent, making it difficult for Playboy to differentiate its product and continue to drive earnings using its reliance on a subscription-based business model. The company did realize economies of scale quickly by finding ways to repurpose content for multiple media, but a fully developed integrated marketing strategy was not yet in place in the 1980s.

The key to future success would be in creating an integrated marketing strategy where Playboy's content could be delivered through multiple categories and to various markets in the most efficient manner and fully leveraging economies of scale. Playboy's integrated marketing strategy was just beginning in the 1980s, and it wouldn't be until the next decade when the company would truly pursue both integrated and vertical marketing strategies (both are discussed in Part V). However, the pieces were being put in place in the 1980s, and the stage was being set for real growth and a resurgence of the Playboy brand in the years to come.

THE BRAND CHAMPION SHOCKS THE WORLD

Playboy Enterprises had been at the center of controversy throughout its lifecycle and at all times Hugh Hefner stood as the one constant. He had become not just the living embodiment of the brand but also the most recognized and influential brand champion and advocate in history. The world would be shocked in July 1989, when the living symbol of the Playboy lifestyle proposed to Playmate Kimberley Conrad. The ultimate icon of the Playboy brand planned to take himself off the market. It's not surprising that Hugh Hefner would make this move in the late 1980s after so many years of living the Playboy lifestyle. After a drug scandal, the Meese Report, lost gambling licenses, failing businesses, closed Playboy Clubs, a stroke, and so on, what is surprising is that Hefner didn't remove himself from the picture much earlier.

The question in 1988 turned not to whether or not Playboy would survive, but to what would happen to the Playboy brand with the brand champion removed from both the daily operations on the business side of Playboy Enterprises *and now* the public side of the Playboy lifestyle? The 1990s would mark a significantly different Playboy. With no visible brand champion, the brand once again struggled to find its identity and a consistent message.

PART V
REINVENTING A BRAND—THE 1990s

TABLE V **Timeline—The 1990s**

1990: Hugh Hefner's first son with Kimberley Conrad, Marston Glenn, is born.

1991: Hugh Hefner's second son with Kimberley Conrad, Cooper Bradford, is born. Playboy Enterprises climbs back to profitability.

1992: A documentary film about Hugh Hefner's life, *Once Upon a Time*, debuts in theaters around the United States and on cable television.

1993: Playboy Enterprises eliminates 10% of its workforce.

1994: Playboy.com debuts. The annual Midsummer Night's Dream Party ends at the Playboy Mansion, and the annual New Year's Eve Party changes from pajamas and negligees to black tie and gowns with children in attendance. Playboy Enterprises ends the year operating in the red again.

1996: Hugh Hefner wins the International Publishing Award from the International Press Directory. *Hugh Hefner: American Playboy* debuts on A&E.

1997: Playboy Cyber Club, a paid Web site, launches.

1998: Hugh Hefner is inducted into the Hall of Fame of the American Society of Magazine Editors.

1998: Hugh and Kimberley Hefner announce their separation. The Playboy Mansion reopens to the public.

1999: Playboy Enterprises acquires Spice Entertainment, Inc. and launches Playboy TV International and Playboy TV en Espanol. Playboy Enterprises signs an agreement to establish the first free-standing Playboy boutique in Japan. Playboy On Campus debuts.

CHAPTER 14

A NEW FOCUS

We went through a period in which both the brand and I were kind of in a tunnel.

Hugh Hefner, 2003 Interview with
the Hollywood Reporter

The 1990s began with a new set of problems for the Playboy brand. With its brand champion, Hugh Hefner, married to Playmate Kimberley Conrad and settling into domestic life, the brand was left without a vocal advocate. Consumers were confused by the inconsistent message being sent by the Playboy brand and its living embodiment. In the early 1990s, Hugh Hefner reinvented himself for the fifth time, but this time it was like nothing anyone had seen before or could have predicted. Former self-reinventions had taken the form of obsessive workaholic and aggressive partier, but the transformation in the 1990s was in stark contrast to the brand message he advocated for the four decades previously.

After Hefner's marriage in July 1989, the Playboy Mansion, a symbol of personal freedom and fun, was quickly turned into a traditional family home. Kimberley Conrad forced Hefner to send his Playmates away, and the doors to the mansion were nearly closed. The free-entry, inclusive system Hefner had loved since the day the Chicago Playboy Mansion opened its doors in 1959 was over. In the 1990s, visitors had to be specifically invited before they would be allowed entry into Playboy Mansion West.

On April 9, 1990, Hugh and Kimberley Hefner welcomed a son into the world, Marston Glen Hefner. One year later, Cooper Bradford

Hefner was born on September 4, 1991. Within a short time, life at the mansion changed significantly. Nudity was banned, the "Playmates at Play" sign was changed to "Children at Play," and toys littered the mansion and grounds.

To make matters worse for the Playboy brand and confuse consumers even more, Hefner denounced his prior way of life calling it desperate and fake. In effect, he was also denouncing the Playboy brand and everything it stood for. It is difficult to retain customer loyalty when the brand champion and its loudest advocate says it's a sham. Hefner, who once hosted *Playboy After Dark*, now made guest appearances on family shows such as *Blossom* and *The Fresh Prince of Bel-Air*. In essence, every part of his life in the 1990s ran counter to the Playboy brand promise.

Changes were also made to the famous events held at the Playboy Mansion. Required attire at parties changed from pajamas and negligees to black tie and gowns, and children were welcomed. Rather than guests searching for eggs with suggestive sayings on them at the Playboy Mansion's annual Easter egg hunt, children searched for traditional Easter eggs at a family-oriented event. Perhaps most confusing to consumers and damaging to the Playboy brand was when Hefner told *People* magazine that he felt his new image would not hurt Playboy because everyone loves a redeemed sinner. He told the press and consumers that his 150,000 word Playboy Philosophy that took him years to complete was being changed to a more positive, family-oriented message reflecting his own move to settle down and become more mainstream. What were consumers to think when the brand champion told them the fantasy life the brand promised was wrong?

HUGH HEFNER RETAINS CONTROL OF *PLAYBOY* MAGAZINE

Despite his veritable disappearance from the public eye and clear shift in thinking from swinging single to honorable husband, Hefner retained control of *Playboy* magazine. The 1990s found Hefner continuing to fight battles, but the battles shifted from equality and sexual liberation to political correctness. A 1994 study at the University of Chicago Research Team called "Sex in America" reported that the majority of Americans led fairly normal and reserved sex lives and believed in monogamy. The current attitudes of consumers matched Hefner's own personal reinvention to a degree, and the content of *Playboy* magazine changed to mirror those preferences.

Playboy was repositioned further from magazines like *Penthouse* and *Hustler* and more in line with *Esquire* and *GQ*. The magazine focused more on quality than it had even during the decade before. The features loyal consumers expected such as the Playboy Interview stayed, but the tone of the magazine became far less political. Instead, the focus was more in line with the original 1950s message of Playboy that concentrated on relationships, lifestyle, and entertainment. Hugh Hefner had always positioned himself as a romantic, and the contents of *Playboy* magazine in the 1990s reflected more of that nature. Articles sought to teach readers that there was a need to understand the relationships between men and women using messages that were popular for the time thanks in part to media and books like John Gray's *Men Are from Mars, Women Are from Venus*, which was published in the same decade. The primary brand message of Playboy in the 1990s was that men should pursue personal freedoms, but do so within the boundaries of accepted traditions.

To many, the new brand message symbolized Hugh Hefner's unwillingness to take responsibility for the brand's promise within the confines of his new marriage. In Hefner's attempt to make the brand message more mainstream and draw a broader audience to Playboy, the magazine tried to be too many things to too many people, and the brand's positioning became confusing. The magazine's content was created to take a neutral position between liberal and conservative thinking. In essence, the brand became a symbol of dichotomies:

- Liberal vs. conservative thinking
- Personal freedom vs. morality
- Sexual freedom vs. quality relationships
- Self-gratification vs. caring for others
- Bachelorhood vs. family man
- Pornography vs. tasteful nudity

The balance would be nearly impossible to find, and throughout the 1990s, consumers would wonder what exactly the Playboy brand message actually was. At the same time, the macro environment in the United States and around the world was changing dramatically. The Cold War was over and true globalization was a reality. Economies around the world were booming and terms such as "tolerance" for prejudiced and inequality became the buzz words that defined the decade in the United States. As early as 1990 when the World Health Organization removed homosexuality from its list of diseases, acceptance became the new norm, and the decade was positioned in stark contrast to decades prior.

In the United States, personal incomes doubled during the decade as political stability and economic development spread further around the globe than ever before, and domestic poverty and crime levels dropped significantly. As women took more high-level roles in the government and private sectors, many of the freedoms Hugh Hefner and the Playboy brand had fought for during the previous four decades had been achieved, at least to a certain extent. Drug use increased in the United States throughout the decade, as did a more open view toward sex with television shows like *Sex and the City* showing the female side of the sexual liberation story.

History books tell the story of changing attitudes toward sex in the 1990s. When former U.S. President Bill Clinton was brought before a grand jury in 1998 to testify about an affair he was accused of having with White House intern Monica Lewinsky, many people were shocked, angry, and embarrassed by his behavior. In the end, he was allowed to remain in office despite his improprieties and less than honest reactions to the accusations, but more interestingly, he remained a fairly popular president.

The fact that many Americans, particularly the members of the younger generation, could look beyond Clinton's sexual deviancy and disconnect that with his role as president was a clear sign of the views people had toward sex at the time. Had the Clinton-Lewinsky scandal occurred a decade earlier, one could argue that the results would have been very different for the president. Of course, it could also be argued that had the scandal occurred at a time when American citizens were feeling less stable economically, politically, and socially, the results may also have been different. However, what will go down in history is the fact that many Americans accepted Clinton's extramarital "sexual relations" and moved on with their lives with little concern.

In short, the 1990s were quite different from the conservative, repressive decade before. In the 1990s, personal freedom and equality were *expected* and people fought against those who didn't comply. The Playboy Philosophy had become outdated and was in need of an overhaul to speak to a new generation who didn't know what it was like to live in the 1950s, 1960s, and 1970s (see Box 14.1 for details about Generation X). *Playboy* magazine wasn't prepared to make the shift necessary to embrace a new generation. Under the editorial leadership of Hugh Hefner, it remained a bit stagnant and boring by consumers' standards in the 1990s. Fortunately, the 1990s also ushered in

BOX 14.1 Generation X

Members of Generation X were born between the years 1965 and 1979. They are the children of members of the Silent Generation and the Baby Boomers. The generation is sometimes referred to as the Baby Bust Generation in reference to the significant drop in birth rate following the baby boom 20 years earlier.

The older members of Generation X were teenagers during the conservative Reagan Years of the 1980s United States. As they reached adulthood, they embraced relationships, community, a focus on the well-being of others, tolerance, and entrepreneurship. At the same time, they denounced the stereotypical Baby Boomer traits of self-centeredness and impracticality. This new generation of adults grew up with a widespread prevalence of broken homes, drugs, AIDS, and globalization. As a result, Generation X focused on recognizing and working to develop awareness and help for the social causes related to the macro environment in which they lived. The 1985 Live Aid concert and attention to issues such as world hunger, environmental protection, and so on were primary concerns for Generation X in the 1990s.

Importantly, Generation X was the first generation to earn less (in real dollars) than their fathers had at the same age. As such, many analysts see Generation X as the generation that believed something had been taken away from them and was owed to them. While previous generations *expected* life to be better for them than it had been for their parents, members of Generation X understood that would not be the case for them. That caused a shift in mindset for Generation X that older generations had trouble understanding. Generation X began to question and rebel against traditions their parents had followed, because they realized the end of the story would not be the same for them as it had been for their parents. They ushered in a demand for flexible work schedules, work-life balance, and more, which the following generation, Generation Y, would continue to champion.

At the same time, technology was advancing at an incredibly fast pace and Generation X was quick to embrace those changes (only to be eclipsed by the early adoption rates of the following generation). Quickly, Generation X demanded the next phase of technology. In other words, Generation X was not satisfied with the status quo and sought ways to make life better through tolerance and social

> awareness, and they worked to achieve those goals through relationship building, community involvement, entrepreneurial thinking, and technological innovation. With the end of the Cold War in the 1980s, Generation X was the first generation to live in a truly global world both socially, politically and economically.

a renewed interest in entertainment and celebrities, two of Hefner's greatest interests, which would give the magazine the relevance it desperately needed and keep it going throughout the decade.

For Playboy, the new Generation X was more difficult to connect the Playboy brand with than any generation before it. This is a generation of Americans that grew up during the conservative Reagan administration but as adults were presented with the problems of an entire world, knowing their economic futures would not be as bright as the generations before them. The challenge in the early 1990s was finding ways to connect the Playboy brand to the personal lives of the members of Generation X. Young Gen X celebrities would play an important role in the latter part of the decade in re-establishing the Playboy brand as modern and relevant for young adults.

CELEBRITIES AND PLAYBOY

Since Playboy's inception, the magazine has had an important relationship with celebrities. Much of that connection came from Hugh Hefner's obsession with movies, which he frequently cited as being his passion from a young age. In the debut issue of *Playboy* magazine in 1953, Hefner hung his hopes of success on a nude image of Marilyn Monroe whose career was rising quickly. It worked, and Hefner never forgot the power of celebrity and its influence on *Playboy*. Over the course of the life of *Playboy* magazine, there were numerous incidences of sales increases corresponding with a well-known celebrity's appearance in a pictorial. In the 1990s, several celebrities stood out as reviving Playboy's popularity to a broader, mainstream audience.

Women like Pamela Anderson and the stars of *Baywatch* became hot commodities as the decade progressed. Anderson had gotten her career break after posing for *Playboy* in 1989, and she was extremely grateful and loyal to Hefner and Playboy overall. She made many appearances in *Playboy* magazine in the 1990s and was coveted by men around the world as the ultimate sex symbol. Playboy marketed her appearances in the magazine heavily and sales rose anytime she graced the pages of the magazine. Other celebrities such as Anna Nicole Smith and Jenny McCarthy launched their careers through *Playboy* and made frequent appearances in the magazine throughout the 1990s. Their popularity soared and magazine sales felt the positive effects. Celebrities such as Drew Barrymore, Shannen Doherty, Farrah Fawcett, Cindy Crawford, Katarina Witt, Naomi Campbell, Claudia Schiffer, and Geri Halliwell of the Spice Girls also appeared in *Playboy* magazine in the 1990s keeping the buzz about celebrities and Playboy alive throughout the decade.

Celebrity appearances in *Playboy* not only appealed to consumers for the content but also for the perceived endorsement of the brand that they carry, particularly among the female audience. When a woman with significant star power posed in *Playboy* magazine, it gave the publication and the brand an image of higher quality and acceptance that many consumers find security in. For example, consumers might think, "If an Olympic athlete like Katarina Witt thinks *Playboy* is okay, then maybe it's okay for me, too." As such, *Playboy* ramped up the number of celebrity appearances in the magazine during the 1990s, particularly with the inclusion of more established celebrities.

Celebrity connections to a brand can be powerful (see Box 14.2 for more examples), and the result for *Playboy* in the 1990s was a renewed interest in the magazine which may have lost even more in terms of circulation numbers during the decade had those celebrities not found their way into the magazine. In many ways, Pamela Anderson, Anna Nicole Smith, and other celebrities breathed new life into *Playboy* in the 1990s and gave it enough momentum to keep going at a time when the brand was struggling to find its message, position, and promise.

BOX 14.2 The power of celebrity brand endorsements

Many consumers, particularly in the United States, are greatly influenced by celebrities. Hugh Hefner, himself, has been considerably influenced by celebrities and Hollywood throughout his life, so it's not surprising that celebrity appearances in *Playboy* magazine can boost sales significantly. However, Playboy is not the only company that leverages the power and reach of celebrities to boost product sales. Following are several other examples:

- *Buick*: When Buick wanted to reposition its old-fashioned brand image and boost sales within a younger consumer segment in the late 2000s, the company enlisted the young golfing pro Tiger Woods to become the face of the brand. Unfortunately, it was an association that most young consumers didn't buy into, and the campaign was not as successful as Buick had hoped.
- *Hanes*: When undergarment manufacturer, Hanes, wanted to steal market share from its competitors in the 1990s and 2000s, the company turned to NBA player Michael Jordan whose wide-reaching recognition and popularity gave the brand a much needed boost.
- *American Express*: When American Express wanted to broaden the audience for its credit card products, the company enlisted a laundry list of celebrities from various demographic backgrounds to appeal to consumers from all walks of life. Celebrities like Jerry Seinfeld, Ellen Degeneres, Kate Winslet, Tina Turner, Dave Matthews, Martin Scorsese, Robert DeNiro, Venus Williams, and more have appeared in *American Express* ads.
- *Tobacco companies*: Celebrity endorsements go back a long, long time. For example, in the 1930s and 1940s, tobacco companies used over 200 celebrities to promote their products, including Clark Gable, Spencer Tracey, Joan Crawford, John Wayne, Bette Davis, Betty Grable, Al Jolson, and more.

PLAYBOY MAGAZINE BY THE NUMBERS IN THE 1990s

Playboy magazine wasn't failing by any stretch of the imagination in the 1990s. In fact, it remained the number one men's magazine for its entire lifecycle. By the end of the decade, Playboy Enterprises reported in its 1999 Annual Report to Shareholders that one in seven men in the United States between the ages of 18 and 34 read *Playboy* magazine. The magazine's rate base (the total newsstand and subscription circulation numbers guaranteed to advertisers) by the end of the decade was still higher than other well-known magazines such as *Sports Illustrated* and *Newsweek* and was ranked 12th among U.S. consumer publications. At the end of the 1990s, the number of advertising pages in

Playboy was growing and as a result, advertising revenues were also on the rise (e.g., a 6% increase from 1998 to 1999).

However, the 1990s did not bring a strong resurgence in *Playboy* magazine circulation, which had fallen from its high of over 7 million copies per month in 1972 to 4.7 million copies per month by 1990. There were several factors working against *Playboy* magazine in the 1990s, and much of the decline, which started 20 years earlier, would not be reversed in the 1990s. The primary factors negatively impacting Playboy in the 1990s were:

- *New competition from "laddie" magazines*: New competition emerged in the 1990s from what the publishing industry referred to as "laddie" magazines such as *FHM* and *Maxim*. While not pornographic, these magazines were erotic, and the modern, timely content appealed directly to the younger male audience.

- *New competition from the Internet*: As the decade progressed, new competition would come from the Internet. Ultimately, much of that competition would be available for free and offered a more interactive experience than the one-dimensional *Playboy* magazine provided.

- *The proliferation of sex*: Sex was everywhere in the United States in the 1990s, and *Playboy* had lost touch with the new generation of adult consumers who could access sexual content from a variety of media at anytime. In short, *Playboy* no longer offered added-value, nor was it differentiated far enough from the competition to make young consumers believe they needed to buy it.

Hugh Hefner responded to falling circulation numbers in the 1990s by revamping *Playboy* magazine again. He hired a new editor away from *Maxim* and tried to create a new version of *Playboy* that stood for a specific type of lifestyle as it had in earlier decades before the conservative 1980s. The goal was to create the next level of men's magazine for younger adult readers who were ready to trade up from *Maxim*.

At the end of the decade, 3.2 million copies of *Playboy* magazine were sold each month in the United States (80% through subscriptions), and two-thirds of revenues were generated from subscription and newsstand circulation. Necessarily, the focus shifted in the 1990s to finding ways to introduce *Playboy* magazine into additional international markets. Global expansion would help Playboy Enterprises build the Playboy brand around the world by opening the path to launch additional Playboy branded products and merchandise once the company gained entry into those regions via *Playboy* magazine (see Chapter 15 for more information about Playboy's international growth in the 1990s).

However, steps still needed to be taken to differentiate the Playboy brand in a highly competitive marketplace and create a perceived need for Playboy products, such as *Playboy* magazine, given the proliferation of freely available, similar content. Again, this would be Playboy Enterprises' biggest obstacle, and the company would never quite find the right way to overcome it. A lack of focus and long-term planning would work against Playboy Enterprises again in the not so distant future.

CHAPTER 15

NEW BRAND EXTENSIONS

We started with the idea that the possibilities were too intriguing for us not to be involved in the online world. We didn't pretend that we knew what the business model was going to be, but we saw a medium with unique properties of interactivity and global reach.
Christie Hefner, Winter 1999 Interview in *ContextMag*

As 1990 began, Hugh Hefner had removed himself completely from daily business operations at Playboy Enterprises. While he still participated in major strategic decisions, his business role in the 1990s was dedicated to editing *Playboy* magazine, although he still retained control of major decision-making, despite his absence. Christie Hefner was given the monumental task to lead the company back to profitability. Throughout the decade, Playboy Enterprises would be rebuilt, but it would never reach the size, strength or profitability that it achieved 20 years earlier. Christie Hefner continued on the strategic path she started in the 1980s wherein Playboy Enterprises worked to refocus the brand on its core competencies and strongest businesses. Primary areas of concentration in the 1990s would be television, merchandising, and the Internet.

With a new brand message of sexiness without being explicit in place, Playboy Enterprises sought to pursue four primary strategies:

1. Expand into global markets
2. Expand television and video segments
3. Expand merchandising
4. Develop an online business

Each of the four strategies listed above is discussed in detail in the remainder of this chapter.

GLOBAL EXPANSION OF PLAYBOY

With the fall of the Berlin Wall in 1989 and the end of the Cold War and Communist regime, Playboy found new markets that were eager for products from the Western world. Throughout the 1990s, *Playboy* magazine debuted in seven former Communist countries expanding the brand's global reach significantly. The Playboy brand was extremely popular in many parts of the world and was even named the most popular foreign brand in China by 2003. Global expansion would be the key to keeping *Playboy* magazine alive in the 1990s and marketing other Playboy branded products and content to consumers around the world. *Playboy* magazine was cited throughout the decade as the catalyst to opening new opportunities for Playboy Enterprises to expand into new countries then extend once the brand secured its foothold in those new international markets.

By the end of 1999, *Playboy* magazine was available in 15 different editions published around the world through international publishing partnerships and licensing agreements and reached a combined circulation rate of 1.5 million copies per month (the German and Brazilian editions accounted for 55% of the total licensing revenues Playboy Enterprises earned from international editions of *Playboy* magazine). Playboy Enterprises followed an international expansion strategy that included partnering with local publishers to create content relevant to each market where the magazine was published while still providing local editions access to publish Playboy-created content. The Playboy brand name brought instant recognition and strength, but Playboy Enterprises was shielded from much of the investment costs and risks.

The end of the decade found the Playboy brand in markets around the world via *Playboy* magazine, television, merchandise, and online. Most significantly, in 1999, Playboy Enterprises completed a joint venture with Cisneros Group to launch Playboy TV International, which would open the doors for Playboy television programming to reach markets outside the United States and Canada. The licensing agreement with Cisneros Group provided cash to Playboy Enterprises and took many of the operational, legal, and other costs out of the company's books.

Additionally, the growing accessibility to Playboy branded content created an increase in demand in global markets for Playboy merchandise. By 1999, 65% of Playboy Enterprises' trademark licensing royalties came from international licenses. That growth was also a catalyst for early success when Playboy Enterprises ventured into the new online world in 1994 with the debut of Playboy.com. By the end of the decade, 25% of the Playboy Web site's traffic came from people outside the United States.

Of course, global expansion didn't come without controversy. Nothing ever does for the Playboy brand. Protests against Playboy were held in numerous countries as the magazine and merchandise debuted, and the brand grew around the world. In fact, several international editions of Playboy failed in the 1990s. However, more survived than exited, and the publishing division of Playboy Enterprises managed to stay profitable throughout the decade despite fluctuating paper costs, higher postage rates, and new online competition.

EXPANDING THE TELEVISION AND VIDEO SEGMENTS OF PLAYBOY ENTERPRISES

During the 1990s, Playboy Enterprises' consistent ray of hope was its entertainment business, including its television, video, and movie businesses. The company spent the majority of the former half of the decade finding ways to gain channel space in cable markets across the United States and slowly, the Playboy Channel grew. With the launch of pay-per-view television in the 1990s, Playboy Enterprises found new ways to sell its television programming content. The company pursued a strategy of providing high quality, original content through various media outlets, much of which was created in the company's own studio in California and reused in other distribution channels such as *Playboy* magazine, Playboy DVDs and videos, and Playboy.com. Providing quality original content, which cable operators could feel confident in, gave Playboy a chance to help those cable operators sell their lucrative pay-per-view services. As such, the Playboy Channel, special sporting events, and big name movies were positioned as the bait by cable operators to encourage consumers to purchase pay-per-view television programming.

When digital cable was introduced, the number of available channels increased significantly, making way for Playboy to increase its distribution reach to more households than ever before. Playboy TV was well-positioned to grow its number of pay-per-view and subscription viewers. In 1999, Playboy Enterprises made significant investments in growing the Playboy entertainment division around the world:

- *Spice*: Playboy Enterprises acquired Spice Entertainment, Inc., which included two cable networks, Spice and Spice 2. The programming was considered to be more hard-core pornographic than the content found on Playboy TV (which Playboy Enterprises promotes as being made for couples) and gave Playboy access to consumers looking for the next step in adult entertainment.
- *Playboy TV Espanol*: The Spanish-language Playboy network was launched within the United States with programming delivered from Playboy's Latin American network.
- *Playboy TV International*: Through a joint venture with Cisneros Television Group, both Playboy TV and the Spice networks would be positioned to launch in new countries.

By the end of the decade, Playboy Enterprises' entertainment division had grown to include:

- Home videos and DVDs sold in 55 countries
- Playboy TV with 25 million household customers
- Playboy TV en Espanol offered to approximately 3 million Spanish speaking households within the United States
- Spice network with 16 million U.S. household customers
- Playboy TV International extending the brand's reach to consumers around the world

Concurrently, Playboy Enterprises was investing millions of dollars into fighting a U.S. law, Section 505 of the Telecommunications Act of 1996 that made cable television restrictions stricter than those applied to print and Internet distribution. That law limited the forms of programming cable operators could deliver to consumers. When digital cable made it possible for cable operators to provide a wider variety of programming to consumers, the restrictions hurt even more. It wasn't until the next decade that Section 505 would be overturned, but Playboy Enterprises earned a lot of points and forged stronger relationships with cable operators from its vocal and financial support in fighting Section 505 (see Box 15.1 for details about Section 505). Once the law was overturned, Playboy TV would face more competition from lower-cost providers who faced fewer entry barriers to the market, as discussed in more detail in Chapter 17.

BOX 15.1 United States vs. Playboy Entertainment Group, Inc.

In the United States vs. Playboy Entertainment Group, Inc. (decided on May 22, 2000), the U.S. Supreme Court was asked to determine whether Section 505 of the Telecommunications Act of 1996 violated the First Amendment of the U.S. Constitution, which guarantees free speech. Section 505 was put in place to counter a phenomenon called "signal bleed" wherein the scrambling of paid cable signals was often imprecise allowing non-paying customers to view fuzzy images and audio of paid channels, such as the Playboy Channel, which distribute content that may be inappropriate for children.

Section 505 required cable television operators that provided channels primarily dedicated to sexually oriented programming to fully scramble or fully block those channels in order to limit children's access to them. Alternately, Section 505 required cable television operators that could not fully scramble or fully block those channels to limit the transmission of them to between the hours of 10:00 p.m. and 6:00 a.m. when children were not likely to be watching television. The majority of cable operators chose to follow the time channeling option, which meant the Playboy Channel was only available between the hours of 10:00 p.m. through 6:00 a.m. As such, many cable operators chose not to carry the Playboy Channel preferring to dedicate channel space to programming that could run all day and drive more revenue. Playboy CEO Christie Hefner said of Section 505, "We felt it was an intrusion on individual choice by the federal government."

Attorneys for Playboy argued that Section 505 was too restrictive, and another provision in the Telecommunications Act of 1996 achieved the same outcome in a much less restrictive manner. Section 504 of the same law required cable operators to fully scramble or fully block any channel a subscriber does not want to receive upon request and without charge. The U.S. Supreme Court ultimately decided with Playboy Entertainment Group stating that a blanket ban was a violation of free speech when a less restrictive alternative was already available. In the Court's decision, Justice Anthony Kennedy, writing for the majority, said, "The Government cannot ban speech if targeted blocking is a feasible and effective means of furthering its compelling interests." Section 505 was overturned and cable operators began delivering content previously regulated under the provision with full scrambling and blocking available upon a subscriber's request.

The entertainment arm of Playboy Enterprises was growing and thriving throughout the 1990s. Although there were obstacles to pass, including legislation limiting adult content on cable television (the aforementioned Section 505), protests against cable operators offering Playboy TV, and more, the entertainment division was on an upswing and became the biggest profit center for Playboy Enterprises for much of the decade. During a time when the Internet was not available in all homes and connection speeds were abysmally slow, Playboy TV and the Spice networks provided some of the only places consumers could experience the Playboy brand and adult content in the privacy of their own homes when they wanted to and on their terms.

Video and DVD sales supported the growth of the entertainment division in the 1990s even more. In 1998, Playboy Home Video found itself included in *Billboard*'s list of the "Top Video Sales Labels" for the fifth year in a row. Playboy videos were available in 55 countries by 1999, and each new video the company released quickly climbed up *Billboard*'s top 40 video sales list. In 1999, all 16 Playboy videos released throughout the year reached *Billboard*'s top 40 list. As DVDs began to take the place of videos, Playboy began releasing existing titles in DVD format in 1997. In 1999 alone, Playboy released over 50 existing Playboy titles on DVD. Videos and DVDs were sold through catalogs, direct mail, *Playboy* magazines, and online at the new Playboy.com store. Additionally, the Playboy Auctions Web site that launched in 1999 provided a perfect place to sell DVDs and videos along with other collectible merchandise. Throughout the decade, Playboy's video and DVD sales continued to grow and thrive.

EXPANDING PLAYBOY MERCHANDISE

During the 1990s, Playboy merchandise brought in a small amount of revenue in comparison to the publishing and entertainment divisions of Playboy Enterprises, however, the brand was a valuable asset that was known around the world. That made it an important piece of the Playboy company's strategy of global expansion. By the end of the decade, over 1,000 specialty stores in the United States and hundreds of international retail outlets carried Playboy merchandise, and in 1999, Playboy Enterprises announced plans to establish the first freestanding Playboy boutique in Japan.

As new markets opened to the Playboy brand, more products and licensing agreements were developed. New product entries, such as

Playboy branded cigars, and new distributors, such as Urban Outfitters, debuted in the 1990s, and the Playboy.com Web site provided a new distribution outlet visible to the millions of consumers who visited each day. By 1999, over 2,700 Playboy-branded items were available through the online Playboy Store and over 3,100 items were available in the online Spice Store.

The latter half of the decade also brought a new audience to Playboy that the brand had not catered to previously. In the late 1990s, it was acceptable for women to like the Playboy brand, too. To capitalize on the rising interest among women toward the Playboy brand, the company launched a new clothing line for women and new jewelry products. In 1998, a new television show for women debuted on HBO, *Sex and the City*, starring Sarah Jessica Parker as a single woman living, working, and navigating relationships in New York City. When Sarah Jessica Parker's character, Carrie Bradshaw, wore a Playboy bunny necklace on *Sex and the City*, viewers noticed, and the unofficial celebrity endorsement made Playboy-branded merchandise even more popular than it was before. This popularity would grow in the 2000s, and Playboy would eventually see its merchandise business grow to become its largest profit center with women responsible for the majority of Playboy merchandise sales.

PLAYBOY ONLINE

The 1990s began with a focus on building Playboy Enterprises' entertainment business, but when a little thing called the Internet became available to the public in 1991, the writing was on the wall that the world was about to change significantly. Companies like Playboy had to re-engineer their business models very quickly to not only secure a Web presence but also to find ways to generate revenue from that presence. Getting online required large up-front investments, and Playboy Enterprises took the steps necessary to become the first magazine with a Web site in 1994. Playboy.com received approximately 150,000 hits during its first week and continued to grow steadily.

The Internet presented another way to distribute Playboy-branded content and merchandise, but it also created new competition. However, it took several years for the majority of homes in the United States and around the world to get access to the Web, and for many years, that access was only available through slow and expensive dial-up connections. Once broadband connectivity became the norm, competition from the online market would grow exponentially, but in the 1990s, it didn't pose a significant threat to Playboy's other lines of business. Again, Playboy Enterprises demonstrated its lack of foresight and long-term strategic planning. Instead of continually analyzing the market; predicting trends, opportunities, and threats; and positioning the Playboy brand for ongoing success, the company complacently allowed it to grow on its own with far less care than it required.

Playboy Enterprises did expand its Web site, Playboy.com, throughout the 1990s. What began as a single Web site grew into multiple destinations, such as the Playboy Cyber Club started in 1997, which was subscriber-based and operated as a Playboy fan club providing more valuable, exclusive content than visitors could access for free on Playboy.com. By the end of the decade, the Playboy Cyber Club had over 40,000 subscribers. The Playboy Store also became an integral part of the Playboy Web site in the 1990s as did the Spice Store to the Spice Web site acquired in 1999. The same year, Playboy launched an auction site to further leverage the online distribution point for Playboy collectibles.

As the decade progressed and the Internet morphed from an informational tool to a transactional tool and finally to an interactive destination, Playboy tried to keep up. Playboy Enterprises added Web chats with Playmates and webcasts of select Playboy special events for Playboy Cyber Club members. Focus in the latter part of the decade turned to creating original content for Playboy.com, finding new ways to make the site interactive and build deeper brand relationships with consumers, and developing a more integrated marketing strategy where the various aspects of the Playboy business could cross-promote and grow organically. In order to achieve that growth, Playboy Enterprises planned to invest significant amounts of money into growing its Web site and Web presence.

Unfortunately for Playboy Enterprises, the growth of the Internet exploded in the new millennium, and what started out as a great new distribution channel turned into the biggest competition the company had ever known. It changed the marketplace. It changed the business landscape, and it changed the majority of companies, including Playboy Enterprises. The key to success going forward would be dependent on how well Playboy's management team could not just respond to those changes but get ahead of the curve in order to dominate its markets in the future.

CHAPTER 16

THE BRAND CHAMPION RETURNS TO THE SPOTLIGHT

We live in a Playboy world today. You see it reflected on television and the Internet, in newspapers and magazines—from shows like Sex and the City, *in which Sarah Jessica Parker wears a Playboy Rabbit Head necklace to Jay Leno's nightly monologue.*

Hugh Hefner, January 2000 interview
in *Playboy* magazine

Since Hugh Hefner proposed to Playmate Kimberley Conrad in July 1988, the Playboy brand champion was absent from the spotlight where, for four decades previously, he had played a significant role in the growth of the company behind the brand. Few other brands in history had such visible and vocal brand advocates and brand guardians as Playboy did in Hugh Hefner. Much of the world saw Hugh Hefner as the living symbol of Playboy and his absence in the 1990s did not go unnoticed by consumers. Furthermore, the highly publicized changes at the Playboy Mansion discussed in Chapter 14, which had long been regarded as Disneyland for adults, added to the confusion and further clouded the Playboy brand message. Hefner's vocal and physical denouncements of the lifestyle he led prior to marrying Conrad in 1989 were heard around the world, and many loyal customers were confused by a brand that struggled with living its own promise in the 1990s.

It was that extended absence that made Hugh Hefner's return to the spotlight in 1998 so significant to Playboy Enterprises. On January 20, 1998, Hugh Hefner and Kimberley Conrad's separation was announced.

> **BOX 16.1** Awards and honors bestowed on Hugh Hefner in the 1990s
>
> (Adapted from PlayboyEnterprises.com)
>
> - **1996**: Hugh Hefner receives the International Publishing Award from the International Press Directory in London, England.
> - **1999**: Hugh Hefner is inducted into the Hall of Fame of the American Society of Magazine Editors. Ironically, Gloria Steinem is inducted at the same time.

Within just a few weeks, Hugh Hefner was spotted at nightclubs with beautiful women on his arms. The living embodiment of the Playboy brand was back and ready to champion the brand again. Hefner spent 1998 reinventing himself for a sixth time.

In April 1998, he was inducted into the Magazine Hall of Fame, reminding the world of his long history with and contributions to the publishing industry (see Box 16.1 for a list of awards Hefner won in the 1990s). At the same time, a new generation of celebrities and customers was learning who Hugh Hefner really was. This new Generation X crowd didn't remember the Hugh Hefner of the 1970s and earlier. They heard stories and saw pictures, but suddenly, the biggest Playboy advocate was showing a new generation exactly why the Playboy lifestyle was so enviable, and why he was the face of that lifestyle, despite his aging outward appearance, and they welcomed his return.

The December 1998 issue of *Playboy* magazine made the re-emergence of the Playboy brand champion complete when it was officially announced that the Playboy Mansion was open again, complete with parties, Playmates, and more. Two years later, in January 2000, Hugh Hefner was the subject of a Playboy Interview where he provided some insight about why his return to the spotlight in 1998 was so well received. Hefner explained, "Timing is everything. If I'd returned a few years earlier, I think I would have encountered a very different response. What I found was a post-feminist, retro world in which young people are ready to party again. I think it's a reaction to the conservatism of the 1980s and early 1990s," (Randall, p. 206).

COMPETITION GROWS

Hefner's return to the public eye gave the Playboy brand a much needed boost and created a strong buzz, but the company was not without its problems in the latter part of the 1990s. The 1970s and 1980s brought fierce competition in the publishing world from hardcore pornographic magazines such as *Penthouse* and *Hustler*. In the 1990s, this competition continued, and new competition came from what the publishing industry refers to as "laddie magazines" such as *Maxim* and *FHM*. Both of these magazines gained considerable attention and momentum in the 1990s as they successfully convinced a long list of young and highly popular celebrities to pose for non-nude but provocative pictorials. Perhaps more significant to the fate of *Playboy* magazine in the 1990s, however, was the *content* of magazines like *Maxim*. While *Playboy* struggled to appeal to a new generation of adult readers, *Maxim*, *FHM*, *Stuff,* and other lad magazines offered the content the coveted young demographic wanted. As sales numbers for lad magazines rose, *Playboy* found itself losing more market share and having more difficulty replacing its aging consumer-base with younger readers.

At the same time, the Internet was growing. Playboy was the first magazine to get online, and being first is always helpful. Typically, the pioneer brand has the opportunity to own a word or *category* in consumers' minds, which can be very powerful. However, the company didn't foresee how fast the Internet would grow nor how it would change the way consumers live. By the end of the 1990s, the Internet wasn't just another business opportunity for Playboy Enterprises. It was also competition for the company's existing businesses. Instead of adding a new way for consumers to experience the Playboy brand, as Playboy clubs, resorts, and casinos had done decades earlier, the Internet became a *better* way for many consumers to experience the brand.

Additionally, Playboy found the competition for online content, particularly pornographic content, to be fierce. Playboy Enterprises created an online business model that derived much of its earnings from subscriptions and payments for exclusive content. It was a business model the company was comfortable with and had achieved success with previously—through magazine subscriptions and television subscriptions. However, as the Internet grew, so did the amount of free pornographic and erotic content that consumers could access without any kind of subscription, commitment, or constraints. As Playboy

Enterprises had so many times before, it found itself stuck in a hole it had dug, at least in part, by its own lack of long-term strategic planning. Unfortunately, competing with free pornographic content online would become a significant challenge for Playboy in the next decade.

LEVERAGING AN INTEGRATED MARKETING STRATEGY

While much of Playboy Enterprises' business was struggling in the 1990s (or on the verge of struggling), the company did make a key decision to further develop its integrated marketing strategy that would help it survive into the new millennium. An integrated marketing strategy is one that leverages a company's core strengths by delivering consistent messages to consumers through various media. At the same time, Playboy Enterprises was able to vertically integrate its businesses, so the integrated marketing strategy could be delivered through various distribution channels. Christie Hefner and her leadership team recognized the need to bring the various business units together to give the brand the focus it desperately needed in the 1990s (see Box 16.2 for more examples of companies that leverage integrated marketing).

> **BOX 16.2 Integrated marketing in business**
>
> An integrated marketing strategy is one where all marketing messages and campaigns deliver a consistent brand image and promise to consumers. Additionally, those consistent messages must be relevant to each consumer and remain so over time. In other words, an integrated marketing strategy isn't one dominated by short-term tactics. Instead, an integrated marketing strategy focuses on long-term strategic growth, economies of scale, and developing brand equity. It's a customer-centric marketing strategy that, when implemented well, can help strengthen relationships with consumers and drive brand loyalty, because all marketing communications used in an integrated marketing communications strategy should focus on marketing directly to consumer needs and desires based on their well-analyzed buying behaviors and thorough segmentation.
>
> Integrated marketing strategies are critical to companies in the 21st century when communication through a wide variety of media

is the norm. With an integrated marketing approach, all messages from various business units, distribution channels, and so on will consistently deliver on the brand's promise and meet customer expectations for it. Additionally, the parent company must take centralized control to not only ensure messaging consistency but also to realize economies of scale. Playboy Enterprises does this through cross-promotion, cross-advertising, repurposing content, and so on.

Another example of a company that leverages integrated marketing strategies is ESPN. The sports network has extended its brand to numerous distribution channels and markets, including television, merchandise, the Internet, sports bars, radio, stores, a sports complex in Walt Disney World in Florida, and more. The ESPN message remains consistent through all business ventures—ESPN is the go-to place for sports. ESPN uses its integrated marketing strategy to cross-promote between businesses, and the company has had great success doing so.

Google is another great example of a company that leverages integrated marketing strategies but in a different way than Playboy or ESPN. Google has its hands in a wide variety of pots in its effort to dominate Internet business. Its flagship product is the Google search engine, but over time, many additional products and services have come and gone under the Google umbrella. The successful ventures remain, such as Google AdWords, Google AdSense, GoogleDocs, Google Blogger, YouTube, Feedburner, and Picasa. Many of these businesses were acquired throughout Google's lifecycle, and therefore, many retain their original brand names. Nevertheless, Google integrates all touchpoints into its overall marketing strategy. Brand messages are consistent across all ventures and cross-promotion is a key factor in Google's success. When consumers log into their Google accounts and use a Google product, they have an immediate sense of security and trust thanks to the vast equity in the Google brand name.

By integrating Playboy Enterprises' marketing efforts across business units and distribution channels, the company could achieve enormous economies of scale. For example, investments in original content could be spread between *Playboy* magazine, Playboy TV, and Playboy.com as the company took steps to repurpose content for multiple channels of distribution. Additionally, special events could be integrated between channels. For example, Playboy Enterprises hosted its first live multimedia event,

Playboy's Club Lingerie fashion show, in 1999. The event was simulcast on Playboy TV and Playboy.com, and the video of the event was sold through the online Playboy store. The same year, Playboy Enterprises produced ten original movies, which where shown on Playboy TV, international Playboy television networks, rented on DVD and VHS through video stores, and sold around the world on DVD and VHS.

Playboy Enterprises' advertising investments directed consumers to one or more distribution channels and often included messages to encourage existing customers to embrace additional forms of content available through alternate channels. On the flip side, Playboy Enterprises offered packaged advertising opportunities to its advertisers. While the company originally sold advertising piecemeal with distribution channels sold separately from one another, as the decade progressed, Playboy Enterprises recognized the value of bundled advertising. By the end of the decade, large companies with well-known brand names took advantage of advertising packages that gave them exposure on both *Playboy* magazine and Playboy.com.

Playboy Enterprises' integrated marketing strategy was a perfect complement to rebuilding the Playboy brand in the 1990s. Integrated marketing communications by definition create a consistent brand message, and they enabled Playboy Enterprises to develop the Playboy brand as a relationship brand that allowed consumers to develop personal connections with it. The experiences consumers preferred in the 1990s may have changed from what was popular in the 1960s and 1970s, but the desire to experience the brand in more ways than on paper through *Playboy* magazine was still evident.

In the 1990s, consumers had a variety of modern ways to connect with the Playboy brand, which opened the brand to a broader demographic. An experiential branding strategy allowed Playboy Enterprises to create targeted marketing tactics and strategies that spoke directly to consumers in different marketing segments. In essence, Playboy Enterprises strived to create a series of brand touch points in both the real world and virtual world that successfully reinvigorated Playboy as a relationship brand.

As discussed throughout this book, a relationship brand is one that allows consumers to take control of their experiences with that brand and benefits from a pull marketing strategy. By listening to consumers' needs for the brand and understanding what experiences they want from the brand, companies are better able to deliver on those needs and wants. Playboy Enterprises made a variety of changes to its marketing strategies in the 1990s to reconnect with consumers who had clearly voiced their changing preferences based on their buying behaviors for Playboy products and services.

As a relationship brand moves to new distribution channels, the potential audience for that brand grows. Playboy Enterprises recognized that the way to connect with a younger demographic in the 1990s was to invest in its Internet presence. The company targeted college campuses with Playboy On Campus, which was launched in 1999. The program was created for one purpose—to grow the Playboy audience among college students. Through Playboy On Campus, students act as representatives of the Playboy brand on their college campuses throughout North America. Duties include promoting the brand, magazine, products and lifestyle. Representatives are expected to report to Playboy about trends and attitudes on their campuses, volunteer at Playboy events, host on-campus promotions, and create marketing plans for their campuses. Playboy On Campus was not an entirely new concept. A similar program existed in the 1960s and 1970s called Man On Campus, but the new Playboy On Campus focused on connecting both male and female, technically savvy college students with the Playboy brand in new ways, which would allow a new generation to experience the brand in the various ways they personally selected.

According to Hugh Hefner in a January 2000 *Playboy* Interview, "Now a whole new generation identifies with Playboy. The magazine's college readership has increased 62 percent since 1995. We have a string of top-selling videos on Billboard, and there are more than 400 Playboy stores and boutiques selling Playboy merchandise on the mainland of China, where the magazine isn't even distributed yet." (Randall, p. 209). Things were looking up for Playboy.

Unfortunately, as the 1990s progressed and the Internet grew in popularity and accessibility, more consumers abandoned *Playboy* magazine and Playboy TV for the free content found online through competitor Web sites than Playboy Enterprises expected. However, an integrated marketing strategy was put in place in the 1990s, and it was a critical component of the company's rebirth in the latter part of the decade and would re-energize the Playboy brand positioning it to regain popularity in the next decade. Playboy was positioned to use its brand equity well in the early part of the 21st century, and the macro environment was prepared to accept the idea of a fantasy lifestyle again. As always, the question would be, could Playboy get out of the way of its own legacy in order to adapt to keep up in the fast-paced world of a new millennium and the even bigger demands of a new audience of young adults—Generation Y?

PART VI

A BRAND RISES BACK TO THE TOP—THE 2000s AND THE FUTURE

TABLE VI **Timeline—The 2000s**

2000: City of Chicago renames the portion of Walton Street where the original Playboy Mansion was located as Hugh M. Hefner Way. An episode of *Sex and the City* is filmed at the Playboy Mansion and features Hugh Hefner as a guest.

2001: The first international Playboy branded Web site launches at Playboy.de. Two online gaming sites debut at PlayboySportsBook.com and PlayboyCasino.com. A wax statue of Hugh Hefner is added to the Hollywood Wax Museum.

2002: First free-standing Playboy concept store opens in Tokyo, Japan. Hugh Hefner receives the Henry Johnson Fisher Award for lifetime achievement from the Magazine Publishers of America.

2003: 50th anniversary of *Playboy* magazine.

2004: The Palms Casino Resort in Las Vegas announces the construction of the Hugh Hefner Sky Villa.

2005: Playboy: The Mansion video game launches. *Playboy* magazine goes digital. *The Girls Next Door* debuts on E! Entertainment.

2006: Playboy Radio debuts on SIRIUS satellite radio. Playboy venue at the Palms Casino Resort in Las Vegas opens. Club Jenna, Inc. is acquired. New online store for women, ShoptheBunny.com, opens.

2007: Playboy store opens in London (first in Europe). PlayboyU.com launches. iPlayboy for Apple iPhone launches. Playboy Island debuts in Second Life. PlayboyGaming.com debuts.

A BRAND RISES BACK TO THE TOP—THE 2000s AND THE FUTURE

2008: 55th anniversary of *Playboy* magazine. Playboy debuts on Twitter.com. Mobile game Playboy Games: Pool Party launches. Mobile reality series, *Interns*, debuts. Playboy Enterprises closes DVD business.

2009: Playboy publishing and online businesses merge into a single division. A revamped Playboy.com Web site is launched. Playboy Manager.com online game launched. Playboy online gaming sites are shut down. Playboy offices in New York City are moved to Chicago. Christie Hefner leaves Playboy Enterprises. Scott Flanders named new CEO of Playboy Enterprises.

CHAPTER 17

A BRAND FOR A NEW GENERATION

Each new generation of readers should be as excited by it as readers were in the 50s.
　　　　　　　　Christie Hefner talking about the Playboy brand
　　　　　　　　　　in a 2003 interview with Charlie Rose

With the start of a new century, Playboy Enterprises began to see the light at the end of a long, dark tunnel. The beginning of the 2000s brought a revived Hugh Hefner back to the spotlight as the ultimate brand champion, and a new generation of consumers was very receptive to his return. At the same time, Playboy TV was thriving and *Playboy* magazine, while much smaller in terms of circulation than it had been 20 years earlier, was still the number one men's magazine. Playboy.com was growing quickly, and an expanding global audience was gaining access to the Playboy brand through a variety of distribution channels.

The new millennium began positively for Playboy Enterprises with its entertainment business steadily increasing revenues, and its online business getting closer to reaching profitability (which would happen in 2002). Playboy licensing deals were also expanding and quickly picking up steam. The decade began with a number of acquisitions positioning Playboy Enterprises to achieve short-term gains, such as the purchase of Spice Entertainment with its television networks and merchandising business. However, as the number of households in the United States with access to digital cable grew in the early 2000s, so did the amount of television competition for adult programming.

A BRAND RISES BACK TO THE TOP—THE 2000s AND THE FUTURE

Digital signals offer more flexible security options, and the turnover of Section 505 of the Telecommunications Act of 1996 (discussed in Chapter 15) meant that adult programming providers had fewer barriers to entry in the changing market. Fewer barriers meant lower cost to entry, which in turn meant, more competitors offering lower quality and more sexually explicit adult programming as well as increased competition for Playboy TV. The Spice networks fit well into the new television environment and the acquisition of Club Jenna Inc. later in the decade helped Playboy remain competitive in the changing marketplace. However, both Spice and Club Jenna offered more hard-core pornographic content than Playboy ever had. While both continued to operate under their own brand names after the acquisition, they ran counter to the Playboy brand promise consumers understood and expected. In other words, the acquisition failed to solve Playboy Enterprises' bigger problems. As the decade progressed, Playboy TV lost some of its momentum and much of its focus.

With the introduction of video-on-demand (VOD), Playboy Enterprises set out to develop a longer-term television strategy that would position Playboy TV as the adult entertainment provider that delivers quality content when and where consumers want it through subscriptions. The business model for subscription video-on-demand (SVOD) was one Playboy was familiar with and had been leaning on for much of its history. By the 2000s, Playboy Enterprises relied on subscription revenues for both its publishing division (two-thirds of revenues from *Playboy* magazine came from subscriptions) and its online business (the majority of revenues from Playboy's Web sites came from subscriptions).

In Playboy Enterprises' online business, the company continued to hope the investment made in 1994 on its Web site would pay off, and by December 2002, the company's online business, now made up of multiple sites, finally reached profitability. While Playboy Enterprises overall was losing money in the early 2000s, not showing profitability again until 2004, the idea of rebuilding the company was not as far out of reach as it once seemed. In fact, the company's momentum was on the upswing, and much of that success was coming as a direct result of Hugh Hefner's return to the spotlight and the renewed interest in the Playboy brand and the lifestyle it represented. Hefner appeared on a variety of television programs such as *Just Shoot Me* and *Entourage* and in advertisements for companies such as Motorola, Ecko, and Carl Jr's. According to the Internet Movie Database (imdb.com), Hefner made 90 television and movie appearances between the years 2000 and 2009 (through January 2009 only), and he appeared twice in an acting role during the same period. Considering the Internet Movie Database lists

156 total television and film appearances for Hefner as himself and 5 total acting roles since 1959, it's evident that his role as a celebrity and the face of the Playboy brand was a key component of the company's marketing strategy in the 2000s. The brand champion was more visible to the younger generation than ever in the 2000s, and that audience found the fantasy lifestyle advocated by the Playboy brand to be very appealing (see Box 17.1 for more information about Generation Y).

The resurgence in popularity of the Playboy brand in the early 2000s opened the doors for Playboy Enterprises to develop a video game that appealed to a younger demographic, *Playboy: The Mansion*.

BOX 17.1   Generation Y

The members of Generation Y (sometimes referred to as the Millenials) were born between the years 1980 and 2000. They comprise the largest generation in American history and are primarily the children of the Baby Boomer and Generation Jones members. The members of Generation Y are distinctly different than any generation before it. The reason for that difference comes down to one word—technology. The younger half of Generation Y is unlikely to know a time when computers and the Internet were not in most homes and before the word "digital" became commonplace. Even the older members of Generation Y grew up in a highly technologically driven world. As such, Generation Y is used to instant access and instant gratification, and they're willing to adopt new technologies very quickly.

The members of Generation Y grew up during a time in the United States that was relatively calm, socially and politically. Members of this generation don't remember the Cold War, the Vietnam War, segregation, or a time when women didn't work outside the home. Members of Generation Y grew up in homes where both parents worked or in broken homes with a single-working parent and these nontraditional family structures became more the norm than the exception. In short, Generation Y is remarkably different from any generation before it. This is the Internet generation and the MySpace generation, and companies led by members of earlier generations, including Generation Jones, Baby Boomers, and the Silent Generation, have trouble relating to this young audience who embrace user-generated content and the social web over other forms of media.

A few years later, a modern, location-based branded entertainment venue would open, reminiscent of the Playboy Clubs that closed over 20 years earlier. The Playboy venue at the Palms Casino Resort opened in 2006 to rave reviews and included clubs, a boutique, a sky villa, and more, offering consumers a variety of new ways to experience the Playboy brand and deepen their relationships with it.

The Playboy venue drew enormous publicity for Playboy Enterprises, and attracted celebrities and guests from around the world. While Playboy originally pursued obtaining its own hotel and casino in Las Vegas, partnering with the Palms, a brand that already resonated with a younger audience through its connection with MTV's *The Real World* and a variety of celebrity appearances, worked out extremely well. Bringing the Playboy brand to the Palms gave it an instant boost among the younger demographic. Furthermore, the Playboy venue at the Palms was frequently featured in episodes of *The Girls Next Door* (discussed later in this chapter), which introduced it to a broader demographic and made it appealing to a larger audience. The Playboy venue is a high margin business that drives significant revenues for Playboy Enterprises (even during the economic downturn of the late 2000s). By 2008, the tables at the Playboy branded casino in the Palms reportedly earned three times as much as any other casino on the Vegas Strip.

Concurrently, Playboy Enterprises was spending considerable time growing its television and publishing presence outside of the United States, but by the mid-2000s, it was undeniably obvious that both businesses were nearing (or long past) maturity. Consumers were increasingly looking to the Internet for products, services, information, communications, entertainment, and brand interactions, particularly the technically progressive members of Generation Y who not only wanted to experience brands in various ways online, when they wanted to, but they also *expected* it. As both Playboy Enterprises' television and publishing businesses struggled, the licensing and online businesses grew. However, by the latter half of the 2000s, the licensing and online businesses began to encounter problems, which were direct results of the macro environment and competition from free content, respectively.

COMPETITION, THE MACRO ENVIRONMENT AND THE GIRLS NEXT DOOR

Playboy Enterprises understood early on that merchandise sales and licensing deals are closely dependent on macro environmental factors, specifically, the economy. When consumers are doing well financially, they have discretionary income to spend, and branded merchandise sells faster and at higher prices. When the economy struggles, consumers are far less likely to open their wallets for a Playboy-branded coffee mug or a trip to visit the Playboy venue in Las Vegas. As the 2000s passed, Playboy found itself more dependent on the income produced from licensing deals. While the company watched subscription and viewer numbers drop for *Playboy* magazine and Playboy TV, merchandise sales grew. What may at one point have been considered ancillary income suddenly became a vital revenue stream during the latter part of the 2000s. Playboy concept stores opened in locations around the world, and Playboy merchandise was available in thousands of retail outlets in the United States. However, when the economy in the United States and economies around the world weakened at the end of the decade, so did Playboy merchandise sales.

Similarly, Playboy Enterprises thought for many years that its television business could be a significant profit driver, but when the television landscape changed from analog to digital and pay-per-view to video-on-demand and Section 505 of the Telecommunications Act of 1996 was overturned, competition grew enormously. The company found its revenue stream diminishing quickly not only as competition grew in the television market but also as more and more consumers abandoned paid television and magazines for free online content.

In the 2000s, pornographic content was easy to find online. Consumers could find almost any kind of sexually explicit content through simple web searches, and they could do so for free. Playboy Enterprises had built an online business model that was reliant on subscriptions (two-thirds of its online revenue). As the amount of freely available online adult content grew, Playboy Enterprises realized that its business model was not prepared to meet that demand. As a result, consumers looked elsewhere, and the revenue Playboy lost from its television and publishing businesses could not be made up in the online market.

Playboy Enterprises made efforts to combat the changing marketplace by offering *Playboy* magazine in digital form in 2005 and redesigning the Playboy.com Web site in 2006 to add significantly more ad space, but those efforts didn't fix the challenges presented by free online content. Additionally, Playboy Enterprises attempted to extend the Playboy brand into online gaming and launched several international Playboy-branded gaming Web sites over the course of the

A BRAND RISES BACK TO THE TOP—THE 2000s AND THE FUTURE

decade. While the company's gaming Web sites were not legally permitted to allow U.S. gambling, the ventures were still very profitable. However, they took the brand in a different direction, away from its focus, which is a mistake the company had already made in the past. Choosing short-term profitability (extending into online gaming) over long-term strategic planning (focusing on core strengths and the primary brand promise) would backfire in the near future (see Chapter 19 for the fate of Playboy's online gaming venture).

Fortunately, the Playboy brand appeal was on the rise and helped control the potential losses that could have been realized in the mid to late 2000s as consumer preferences and demand shifted. In 2003, *Playboy* magazine celebrated its 50th anniversary with a wide variety of events, parties, special features and editions, and more. The celebration was integrated into all Playboy businesses and drove a great deal of buzz and excitement. In November of that year, Hugh Hefner hosted a television special about Playboy on the A&E network. The 50th anniversary celebration brought a significant amount of press to Playboy Enterprises. Both supporters and critics recognized Hefner and Playboy as catalysts for advancing individual freedoms and directly impacting the lives of Americans. It was just the kind of publicity Playboy Enterprises needed.

The following year, Playboy Enterprises returned to profitability, and the company continued to extend the brand into new international markets through publishing, television, online, merchandise, and mobile and wireless products and services. In the mid-2000s, Playboy Enterprises made several highly focused brand extensions. Playboy was brought to satellite radio via SIRIUS in 2006, and a new online store dedicated to women, ShoptheBunny.com, launched in 2006. Additionally, Playboy Enterprises made a strong push to further connect with specific demographic groups in the 2000s by debuting a number of niche Web sites and online clubs, such as PlayboyNet Espanol for Spanish-speaking Americans.

In another attempt to help audiences around the world connect with the Playboy brand in a new way, Playboy Enterprises prepared to launch a new reality television show in 2005, which was created and produced through its own studio, Alta Loma Entertainment, and broadcast on E! Entertainment. The new program was called *The Girls Next Door* and followed the lives of Hugh Hefner's three girlfriends who lived with him in the Playboy Mansion. The show was an instant hit, particularly among the female audience, and became the most popular show on the E! network.

The Girls Next Door was a genius marketing tactic. The show highlighted many aspects of the Playboy brand promise with a focus on Playboy events, parties and more, which clearly depicted the free and fun Playboy lifestyle for both men and women. Hugh Hefner made frequent appearances on *The Girls Next Door*. As the ultimate brand champion, he appeared to not only be an obsessive workaholic, deeply involved in the magazine and brand, but he also seemed to truly live the brand promise in every way. Celebrity appearances were also common, which added to the timeliness of the program.

The Girls Next Door appealed to audiences in multiple generations, which helped Playboy Enterprises find new ways to connect with the coveted younger demographic as well as a female audience (70% of viewers were women). For example, a new Playboy U social networking Web site debuted in 2007, taking Playboy On Campus, which enlisted college students to represent Playboy on college campuses across North America since its debut in 1999, to the next level of interactivity. Playboy U was developed as a place where college students could communicate, share, upload photos and videos, and become further connected to the Playboy brand through its editorial content devoted to advising people about how to maximize their college experiences. It was an intelligent, focused, and relevant extension of the brand to a targeted, niche audience. The younger male and female demographic was already highly involved in online social networking as the popularity of Web sites like MySpace and Facebook demonstrated in the 2000s. Playboy U provided the next step from MySpace for a niche audience of men and women.

Furthermore, Playboy Enterprises expanded into new distribution channels such as mobile and online virtual worlds near the end of the decade. iPlayboy for the Apply iPhone debuted in 2007 as did Playboy Island in the online world of Second Life. A year later, Playboy joined the microblogging craze by starting a Twitter profile and debuted its first mobile game, Playboy Games: Pool Party, and its first mobile reality series, *Interns* (see Box 17.2 for more information about *Interns*). In 2009, Playboy launched Playboy Manager.com, a Massively Multiplayer Online Role-Playing Game (MMORPG), in an effort to duplicate the success of similar games such as World of Warcraft. These new marketing tactics supported Playboy Enterprises' strategy of appealing to a new generation of consumers and leveraging integrated marketing.

By offering multiple ways for consumers to experience the Playboy brand through digital content, younger consumers found ways to self-identify with the brand in the 2000s. While Generation Y might be unlikely to pick up a magazine, they are highly likely to look to their

BOX 17.2 *Interns*

On December 9, 2008, Playboy Enterprises launched its first mobile reality series, *Interns*. In less than one month, *Interns* received 891,000-page views on PlayboyMobile.com and its distribution partners such as MySpace.com. The premise of *Interns* is similar to Donald Trump's popular television reality show of the 2000s, *The Apprentice*. In *Interns*, three twenty-something interns (two male and one female) at the former New York City offices of Playboy are followed in episodes launched weekly over the course of six weeks. The interns were required to perform a variety of tasks, interact with Playmates, and more.

The key to the success of *Interns* was the research and planning that went into the series prior to its launch. The Playboy Mobile team spent time analyzing mobile-consumption habits, the best ways to film the series, and the right pace for short "mobisodes." Playboy Mobile even went so far as to incorporate product placements into *Interns* episodes. To create a buzz for *Interns* among the young target audience, Playboy used online banner ads and videos, email, mobile banner ads, SMS messaging, Playboy Radio (on SIRIUS), and personal marketing tactics through the company's Playboy On Campus representatives across the United States.

Interns was the product of two primary strategies: broadening the Playboy customer base to appeal to a younger demographic and providing new ways for consumers to experience the Playboy brand through alternate digital distribution channels. At a time when the majority of mobile content was still repurposed video originally created for different media distribution, Playboy made a bold move to create original mobile content based on real research. It was a step in the right direction for Playboy Enterprises, particularly in connecting with Generation Y.

computers or mobile phones to experience a brand like Playboy. With the strong brand value of Playboy paired with modern, experiential marketing, Playboy was positioned to become a strong relationship brand for a new, younger audience. However, history was bound to repeat itself, and by the end of the first decade of the new millennium, Playboy Enterprises was faced with devastatingly low stock prices and rumors of bankruptcy.

CHAPTER 18

A RELATIONSHIP BRAND HISTORY IN REVIEW

[The Playboy brand] is clearly the most valuable asset we have, although it's not reflected on our balance sheet. It only has become more valuable because the fragmentation of media has meant that the recognizable and trustworthy qualities of a strong brand break through the clutter, whether that's on the newsstand, on a 500-channel television system or on the World Wide Web, where there are millions of sites.

Christie Hefner, December 2000 Interview
with *The Wall Street Journal*

The start of a new century placed Playboy Enterprises in a positive position. The resurgence in the brand's popularity among a new generation boded well for the company's short-term growth. However, that growth would be short-lived. Much of the turnaround would occur due to a changing macro environment and rapid technological developments that caused consumers to shift their preferred distribution methods faster than Playboy Enterprises was prepared to handle. Those technological developments opened the doors for increased competition from low-cost providers, which Playboy Enterprises did not foresee. In short, Playboy Enterprises found itself in a reactionary position again, trying to catch up with new competition and the world that was quickly changing around it.

Despite the company's struggles in the 2000s, its story of building brand value is an important one, and it's a history that all marketers

A BRAND RISES BACK TO THE TOP—THE 2000s AND THE FUTURE

can learn from. Throughout the Playboy brand's lifecycle, Hugh Hefner has remained at the center playing three important roles:

1. *Brand Champion*: Hugh Hefner is the ultimate brand champion. He is the face of the brand and truly wants everyone around him to embrace the brand's message, image, and promise with him. Consumers feel the enthusiasm for the brand from him and can't help but feel it, too.

2. *Brand Guardian*: Hugh Hefner tirelessly defends the Playboy brand. Throughout the more than half a century that the brand has lived, Hefner has retained control of major strategic decisions, ensuring the brand goes in the direction he wants it to. Of course, those decisions were not always the best ones, but nevertheless, he protected the brand with vehemence.

3. *Brand Advocate*: Hugh Hefner is a vocal brand advocate for the Playboy brand. He lobbies for its promise and promotes it continually. Whether he's in front of a court of law or the court of public opinion, Hefner doesn't waver in his pursuit of furthering the Playboy brand message, image, and promise.

Hugh Hefner and Playboy are intertwined, and in the eyes of consumers, they are one and the same. Hefner reiterates that connection. In Steven Watts's 2000 biography of Hugh Hefner, *Mr. Playboy*, Hefner says, "The magazine has always been an extension of my own dreams and fantasies" (p. 447). The public sees that relationship, and consumers want to have that relationship, too. In other words, they want to live like Hugh Hefner. They want to live the Playboy brand promise.

Few companies can say they have a single brand champion who guarded and advocated the brand so clearly, and for such a long time, as Playboy can with Hugh Hefner (see Boxes 18.1 and 18.2 for further discussion about well-known brand champions). It's an enviable position that can drive a brand's power to new heights, and Hugh Hefner played the role nearly perfectly throughout the half century plus since *Playboy* magazine launched.

In the January 2009 issue of *Playboy* magazine, the 55th anniversary edition, Hugh Hefner's teenage sons, Marston and Cooper, were interviewed. The article symbolized a precursor to passing the Playboy torch to the next generation of Hefners. The same month, Christie Hefner stepped down from her role as Chairman and CEO of Playboy Enterprises, paving the way for Marston and Cooper to take

BOX 18.1 Steve Jobs: The Apple brand champion

In 1976, Steve Jobs cofounded Apple, Inc. Over the next ten years, he played an integral part in developing the Apple brand and product line, but when an internal battle arose in 1985, Jobs was asked to resign and leave the company he created. Between 1986 and 1993, Apple stumbled. The company's stock plummeted by the mid-1990s after a series of unsuccessful product launches, and a growing list of lower-cost competitors posed increasing threats and challenges. Apple was not positioned to withstand competitive attacks. In 1997, Steve Jobs was named CEO of Apple again, and within a short time, returned the company to profitability and rebuilt the company's brand into one of the strongest brands in the world by the turn of the century.

Steve Jobs is directly credited with much of Apple's success in the late 1990s and early 2000s. Through his public role as brand champion, he has become a celebrity and is inextricably connected to the Apple brand. For example:

- When a false report stating that Steve Jobs suffered a massive heart attack appeared online on October 3, 2008, Apple's stock dropped by 5.4%.
- When Apple announced on December 30, 2008, that Steve Jobs would not attend the annual MacWorld event the following month, Apple's stock fell by 4.5%.
- When Steve Jobs announced on January 14, 2009, that he was taking a 6-month medical leave of absence from Apple, the company's stock price dropped by 10% on the same day.

Consumers and stockholders remember what happened to Apple after Steve Jobs left in 1985. They also credit Apple's turnaround in the 1990s on Jobs's return to the company in 1997. He is tied directly to innovation and creativity in the minds of the public, and he is the face of the Apple iPod, which changed the portable media player market when it debuted in 2001, and the Apple iPhone, a product that redefined the mobile telephone market in 2007.

Consumers, analysts, and shareholders hold varying opinions on the fate of Apple without Steve Jobs as the leader, both as CEO and brand champion. Clearly, his connection to Apple in people's

A BRAND RISES BACK TO THE TOP—THE 2000s AND THE FUTURE

minds can have an effect on the company, as the drop in stock price demonstrated when he announced his leave of absence. Unfortunately for Apple, there is no similar successor in place to take on the role of brand champion in the same way that Steve Jobs has lived it.

BOX 18.2 Mary Kay Ash: The Mary Kay brand champion

Mary Kay Ash started Mary Kay Cosmetics in 1963 with a $5,000 investment. She led her company and acted as brand champion until her death in 2001. Since that time, her office at the Mary Kay Cosmetics building in Dallas, Texas, has remained unchanged (not even the restroom has been used). With the brand champion's death, Mary Kay the company remained frozen in time.

In the late 2000s, the company began implementing a plan to reposition the Mary Kay brand to live again without its brand champion. Doing so has worked and the company is growing again. The company attributes much of its recent success to delivering value-added experiences to consumers, particularly through the MaryKay.com Web site. In 2009, the company conducted extensive research to determine exactly what women want in specific areas of their lives. The results would drive future strategic planning decisions. Of particular importance was the plan to develop new messaging around the strong Mary Kay brand to appeal to existing and new consumers in the mature cosmetics market.

Mary Kay Cosmetics shifted from being stuck in the past due to the loss of its brand champion, Mary Kay Ash, to being focused on the future. The marketing team now develops products by analyzing two to three years into the future in order to predict trends and changes in consumer behavior and preferences. Doing so allows the company to make the necessary adjustments throughout the organization to remain competitive. In other words, the company has shifted its strategy from one focused on short-term sustainability and a reliance on a brand champion to one that concentrates on long-term growth and a reliance on meeting consumer needs for the brand, and it's working.

A RELATIONSHIP BRAND HISTORY IN REVIEW

> **BOX 18.3** Awards and honors bestowed on Hugh Hefner in the 2000s
>
> (Adapted from PlayboyEnterprises.com)
>
> - **2001**: Hugh Hefner is inducted into the New York Friars Club as an honorary Friar.
> - **2002**: Hugh Hefner is named Harvard Lampoon's Best Life-Form in the History of the Universe
> - **2002**: Hugh Hefner receives the Henry Johnson Fisher Award, the Magazine Publishers of America's highest honor.

the leadership roles in the future. Hugh Hefner has stated that both young men have expressed interest in leading the company in the 21st century, and it's expected that once they finish college, they should make the transition to live the legacy set before them.

Marston and Cooper are members of Generation Y. It's highly likely that a new generation of leadership like theirs could push Playboy Enterprises in the direction it has needed to go in for so long but has yet to find. Both young men have indicated that they'd like to take the brand and the magazine back to its roots in terms of creativity and differentiation. It remains to be seen if they'll have the chance, but one thing is for certain, they have big shoes to fill in terms of being Playboy brand champions like their father before them. In the 2000s, Hugh Hefner remained more popular, successful, and talked about (see Box 18.3 for a list of awards Hefner received in the 2000s) than ever.

DEVELOPING A BRAND

No one knew in the early days that the Playboy brand would grow to become one of the strongest brands in the world. However, the pieces were in place to open the path for success. First, Hugh Hefner was in position as brand champion, brand guardian, and brand advocate. Second, the product fulfilled an existing consumer need, and third, the brand invited personal connections with consumers. Through consistent messaging, creating a clear brand promise, and meeting consumer expectations time and again, the Playboy brand would grow quickly.

A BRAND RISES BACK TO THE TOP—THE 2000s AND THE FUTURE

In the 1950s, the Playboy brand appealed to a specific audience of consumers who believed in the messages found on the pages of *Playboy* magazine. They could personalize the lifestyle that *Playboy* advocated, which allowed them to connect with the brand. The audience of consumers who connected with the brand became their own society. Together, they could talk about the brand messages and promise, share information, and deepen their relationships with it and with each other. By the 1960s, Playboy was a strong cult brand with a societal base.

As more and more consumers experienced the brand and found ways to personally connect with it in their own lives, Playboy became an even more powerful relationship brand—every brand manager's ultimate goal. A relationship brand is strong and develops only after consumers develop a powerful, emotional involvement with it. The more emotionally involved a consumer becomes with a brand, the more often they'll buy that brand, choosing it over any other brand, and eventually, advocating that brand to other consumers. This is the path to customer loyalty and word-of-mouth marketing that can carry a brand to the next level of success. Vocal consumer brand advocates can have a significant effect on publicity and sales, and the Playboy brand benefited from the loyalty of its consumers throughout its lifecycle. From the early days through the 2000s, most of the company's revenues had been derived from loyal consumers through subscriptions—for the magazine, television networks, and online.

Customer loyalty is an integral part of the success of Playboy Enterprises overall. To further develop that loyalty, the company has relied heavily on experiential marketing over the years. The strategy is a good one, and many media companies use it. Since the Playboy brand is dependent on emotional involvement, it makes sense to provide a variety of ways for consumers to experience the brand and the messages and promise it delivers. Playboy Clubs were a perfect brand extension in the 1960s and provided a great way for consumers to deepen their emotional connection to the Playboy brand. In later years, *The Girls Next Door* created an excellent way for both men and women to further connect with the brand. In other words, as the world and consumers evolve, so must brand experiences.

Successful experiential marketing begins with providing branded experiences that enhance customers' lives. Immersive experiences, such as the Playboy Clubs or the more modern Playboy venue at the Palms Casino Resort in Las Vegas, allow consumers to live the brand promise in their own ways and bring them closer to the brand. Experiential marketing should engage consumers and encourage them to carry those experiences to the next brand offering. A stand-alone experiential marketing event is not effective. Rather, experiential marketing must be a component of a larger marketing plan where consumers are given the opportunity to connect with the brand and live the brand promise in a variety of ways. Experiential marketing is a customer-centric, 360-degree marketing strategy wherein each consumer in the target market is surrounded by brand choices and experiences from which he can choose in order to take control of his relationship with the brand. In other words, the experiential marketing tactic deepens the strength of a relationship brand, but it does not make a relationship brand in and of itself. Instead, relationship brands develop over time as consumers engage with the brand in multiple ways and take control over how they want to experience the brand in the future.

The key to successful experiential branding is giving consumers control of the experiences. Playboy Enterprises understands that necessity, as Christie Hefner stated in a 2008 interview with *In Business Las Vegas*, "A brand is something that reflects a point of view or an attitude. As such, it can be transferred from one project to another because consumers pick it out as a way of self-identifying with that attitude." The strategy of Playboy Enterprises has been to create a variety of brand touch points, so consumers can decide how they want to connect with the brand and the brand's promise. In other words, Playboy starts the conversation or invites consumers in using its inclusive promise, and then allows them to make their own decisions and connect with the brand in their own ways. Allowing consumers to become emotionally involved in a brand on their own terms is a powerful strategy that has worked for Playboy Enterprises for over 50 years. It's when the relationship brand relies on push marketing strategies instead of listening to customers and allowing them to define the route and pull the marketing choices from the brand that it gets in trouble.

EXTENDING A BRAND

The quick success of the Playboy brand drove Hugh Hefner to extend it into new markets and categories pursuing a haphazard strategy that relied little on research and more on instinct (or personal preferences). Hefner's interest in Hollywood and celebrities led him to extend the Playboy brand into film, television, and music very early in the brand's lifecycle. Playboy also owned a modeling agency, limousine company, and more.

A BRAND RISES BACK TO THE TOP—THE 2000s AND THE FUTURE

Some of the early brand extensions provided consistent brand messaging opportunities, but others were opportunistic and shortsighted.

Over the course of the Playboy brand lifecycle, the Playboy company would extend the brand into more businesses such as Playboy clubs, resorts, casinos, and so on. Typically, rapid overexpansion of a brand can dilute it in the minds of consumers, but for Playboy, the result was a bit different. Many of the company's early brand extensions were successful, but by the 1970s, Playboy had stepped far out of its area of expertise. Not only was the company operating outside of its core competencies, but it was also confusing consumers who had difficulty linking the brand's promise to a myriad of unrelated brand extensions.

In the 1980s and 1990s, under the leadership of Christie Hefner, Playboy Enterprises made a major commitment to refocus the brand and contract it back down to its core competencies. It was an important strategy that was essential to ensuring the brand would live to the next century. The Playboy brand's position as a provider of quality information related to men's interests returned, and the brand's promise was clear again. With clearer focus, Playboy Enterprises was able to develop an integrated marketing strategy among its contracted businesses that repositioned it as a market leader.

Playboy Enterprises' integrated marketing strategy along with the power of the Playboy brand are the two strongest components of the company's future success. Throughout the 2000s, the company has worked to find ways to leverage economies of scale and develop branded products and distribution channels that deliver consistent quality and messaging which meet consumer expectations for the brand. New distribution channels and products have been launched to attract younger consumers and consumers from broader demographics, and the brand remains extremely popular and strong. Playboy Enterprises is finding ways to integrate its many offerings more seamlessly, but there is much work to be done. The company's performance still does not reflect the value of the Playboy brand.

A BRAND COMES FULL CIRCLE

After 50 years in business, the Playboy brand entered the new millennium closer to where it started than anyone could have expected. The focus in the 2000s has been on the Playboy brand, itself, and leveraging its strength to rebuild Playboy Enterprises. By going back to the brand's roots and concentrating on building relationships with consumers and allowing them to experience the brand in the ways they choose, Playboy points to the inherent lifestyle promise of the brand as its success model. The question that remains to be answered is whether or not that's enough to keep Playboy alive for 50 more years.

CHAPTER 19

THE FUTURE OF THE PLAYBOY BRAND

There is definitely more competition or clutter in the marketplace, but no matter how much money I gave you, you couldn't build brand equity like that enjoyed by Playboy today.

Christie Hefner, January 2008 Interview
with *Leaders Magazine*

As the first decade of the 2000s neared its end, Playboy Enterprises existed as a mid-size communications and entertainment company with questionable growth expectations. Its stock price dropped in 2008 to a record low (as did many other companies' stocks due in part to weak economies around the world negatively affecting all aspects of business). It was a position the company had been in before in 1976 when its stock price dropped to just $4 per share. While the Playboy Enterprises' stock price was falling in the late 2000s and many other men's magazines were folding or being sold, the Playboy brand remained strong. In fact, the Playboy brand was experiencing a resurgence in popularity that Playboy Enterprises could leverage to stay afloat and strategize for the future.

Since its debut in 1953, *Playboy* magazine has been the top men's magazine in the world, and Playboy Enterprises uses that position as a stepping stone to extend the Playboy brand into new categories and markets. In the 2000s, the company has followed a strategy of being a high-tech, high-touch brand, meaning it tries to stay ahead of the curve in new media and offer a variety of brand experiences that leverage new technology. Unfortunately, the company is always a bit more reactive than proactive. For example, in 2009, Playboy Enterprises revamped Playboy.com to more closely integrate the Web site with *Playboy* magazine and to include more interactivity, more ad space, and more opportunities for consumers to connect with the brand. It's a change that should have been done several years earlier, but at least it was finally made. In an article by Greg Burns that appeared on the *Chicago Tribune* Web site on January 30, 2009, the new editorial director of *Playboy* magazine and the Playboy Web site was quoted saying the newly redesigned Playboy.com would bring the magazine's "DNA to sight, sound and motion." He reported that the new Web site would "own" animation as well as create "controlled chaos" and "capture lightning in a bottle." New online content including instructional videos (some about sex) and more would also be launched in order to take the Playboy Web site to the next level of consumer brand experience. Only time would tell if the changes would be enough to re-energize Playboy Enterprises.

Additionally, Playboy Enterprises closed its offices in New York City in 2009 in order to consolidate its online and publishing divisions. In a memo to Playboy Enterprises employees dated October 15, 2008, Christie Hefner told employees that the company would "respond to changes in how consumers access content and advertisers use media. Thus, we will continue to deliver more of our content digitally, using our assets across multiple distribution platforms and adding more a la carte offerings." Again, these are changes that simply took too long to come. Christie Hefner all but admitted to Playboy's reactionary management style when she wrote in her memo that the company would "respond" to changes. The most successful companies don't just respond to changes, they anticipate them.

Playboy has made some good decisions in the 2000s. For example, the company launched its first mobile program in 2008, *Interns*, to connect with a younger demographic and made strong pushes to attract the college audience through PlayboyU.com, events and merchandise. For example, several CDs of dance music mixed by popular DJs were released in the United Kingdom to create brand buzz in the region among a younger consumer audience. Similarly, Playboy sought to engage a broader demographic audience, including women and couples, and developed television programming, merchandise and an online storefront that appealed to new consumer segments.

The company's problems at the end of the first decade of the 21st century were three-fold. First, Playboy Enterprises moved slowly. Yes, it was the first publication to launch a Web site, but it was slow to recognize changing consumer preferences and develop ways to meet

A BRAND RISES BACK TO THE TOP—THE 2000s AND THE FUTURE

consumer needs. Second, Playboy Enterprises remained short-sited. For example, the popularity of *The Girls Next Door* and the fact that the majority of Playboy-branded merchandise sold in the 2000s was in the women's fashion or accessories categories proved that the 2000s was the decade of women and Playboy, but the company was slow to leverage the buying power of that audience. Third, Playboy Enterprises was the victim of its own short-term success time and again. When a tactic worked, the company would ride it out with little long-term planning, including exit strategies. Again in the 2000s, the Playboy brand was extended into a myriad of businesses, despite the company's attempts to position it as a focused brand. With a presence in businesses as disconnected as online gaming and car racing, there was still a lack of focus just as there had been in prior decades. When the economy weakened in the late 2000s, and Playboy's online gaming ventures were not driving the revenues the company expected and needed, Playboy Enterprises announced it would close its online gaming sites in January 2009 with less than one month's notice. It was a step in the right direction to focus the Playboy brand, but ironically, the decision was made just when a new president took office in the United States leading many people to anticipate a change in online gaming laws that would open the doors for U.S. consumers to participate and increase both the reach and potential revenues for site owners.

Furthermore, Playboy Enterprises could be accused of using its brand as a crutch. The company relies heavily on the strength of its brand as its most valuable company asset, but it's an intangible asset. While immeasurably useful, it does not drive revenue by itself. The company needs to offer products and services that meet consumer needs and consistently deliver on the brand's promise, or the brand is meaningless. There have been many powerful brands over the course of history that have risen to the top, and then disappeared. For example, some car brands that met their demises with little consumer backlash include Oldsmobile, Plymouth, Datson, and GEO. While brands that disappeared may have been missed for a short time, consumers moved on quickly to find replacements. There is more to a brand than awareness, recognition and trust. The brand has to deliver by differentiating itself from anything else on the market and providing something of value to consumers. That's where Playboy Enterprises struggles time and again after the brand reached maturity—in quickly and effectively delivering products and services that consumers can't live without.

Playboy Enterprises is faced with more competition in the 21st century than ever before, particularly in the form of free online content and looser restrictions related to television content. With its strong brand recognition, and its resurgence in popularity among men, women, young, and old consumer segments, Playboy is in a unique position. There are a wealth of opportunities within reach if Playboy Enterprises is prepared to launch a full-scale rebranding campaign. The world has changed, but the overall Playboy brand image is still tied to a specific male audience. For future growth, the company needs to reposition Playboy as a brand that welcomes everyone.

In other words, Playboy needs to remember its roots as an inclusive brand that invites everyone to the party. However, the messages for the audience of the 21st century are quite different from those used in the 1950s. For example, the late 2000s were overshadowed by a weak economic climate, but eventually, consumers will find themselves with additional discretionary income to spend. A repositioned and revamped Playboy fantasy lifestyle could be a welcome distraction from the hard working lifestyles most consumers live. Reminding consumers they deserve time to play, regardless of what they do in their "real lives" is a timeless message. A modernized version of the original Playboy value proposition, the good life people deserve, is timeless. Offering cutting-edge, experiential marketing in various media will allow consumers to develop personal, self-selected relationships with the Playboy brand.

Naturally, there is not a single strategy that can revive Playboy's financial situation in the 21st century. The above is just one example of how rebranding Playboy could help reposition it for future success. The important thing to understand is that Playboy Enterprises sits in an enviable position, simply because it operates under one of the most recognized brands in the world. The future can hold a world of opportunity, but strategic steps must be taken to rebuild the company. That means focusing, understanding consumers, and delivering value. Simply relying on the power of the Playboy brand isn't enough anymore.

In the 21st century, when consumers have access to incredible amounts of information and technology, Playboy Enterprises needs to build the connection between its brand and individual consumer segments more so than ever before, and it must do so through interactive, experiential marketing that allows consumers to take control of the brand. Playboy must compete for both mindshare and "timeshare" in the 21st century, meaning the brand has to find a place in consumers' minds despite the clutter they face each day, and it must find a place in consumers' very busy schedules for them to interact with it each day.

It's a two-pronged marketing approach that is jump-started thanks to the strength of the Playboy brand. In short, the Playboy brand in the 21st century must be *used* as much as it is *known*.

HUGH HEFNER—THE ULTIMATE BRAND CHAMPION

At the heart of everything Playboy does and stands for is the ultimate brand champion, Hugh Hefner. Analysts and journalists report mixed feelings about the man who created the Playboy brand and became its living embodiment. This is particularly true in the 21st century when Hefner surpassed 80-years old. Many criticized Hefner as being the reason that Playboy Enterprises was stuck in the past and no longer relevant to younger audiences. However, there was no denying the fact that he remained popular even among young celebrities. Famous Generation X and Generation Y faces such as Leonardo DiCaprio, Paris Hilton, Toby Maguire, and Jessica Alba were seen at parties at the Playboy Mansion and in the pages of *Playboy* magazine. Clearly, the younger generations were still fascinated by Hugh Hefner and were attracted to the Playboy lifestyle he embodied. The problem lies in the rapidly changing preferences, behaviors, and demands of younger generations who are used to the instant access and instant gratification that technology delivers and makes available anytime and anywhere. That's the gap Playboy Enterprises needs to overcome.

In an interview with Hugh Hefner and Kimberley Conrad's sons, Marston and Cooper, that appeared in the January 2009 issue of *Playboy* magazine (the 55th anniversary edition), the young men made it clear that they would be the successors to Hugh Hefner in leading Playboy into the future. Christie Hefner stepped down from her role as CEO the same month, and in June 2009, Scott Flanders was named the new CEO. Clearly, a succession plan was in place as far as Hugh Hefner was concerned, but how will the ultimate brand champion's eventual exit affect Playboy overall?

There is perhaps no other brand in the world that has been so closely aligned with one person for such a long time. Hugh Hefner and Playboy are unique in that they are one and the same in many ways. The connection was intentional on Hugh Hefner's part. From the beginning of his reign as the ultimate brand champion, he made it clear that what readers found on the pages of *Playboy* magazine was an extension of his own life, dreams, and fantasies. Conversely, Hefner made it equally clear that his life was a direct attempt to live that fantasy life and to show readers that the dream could be within their reach. As Hefner stated in a March 2008 interview with MarketWatch.com, "From the beginning, it was never a business. If I sold it, my life would be over." In fact, Hefner revealed in a June 2009 interview with *Los Angeles Confidential* magazine that his only true business regret was taking Playboy public. Hefner said, "I think the company would have been closer to home if it had remained a private corporation." Most business analysts would agree with that statement. Despite making that mistake, Hefner was able to retain a great deal of control over the brand he created and lived.

Clearly, Hugh Hefner plans to stay in his role as the ultimate brand champion for Playboy for as long as possible. Arguments could be made from both sides of the fence—it's a good thing or it's a bad thing. Whichever side of the debate one finds himself on, one thing has been certain for over half a century—Hugh Hefner is Playboy, and Playboy is Hugh Hefner. Can one survive without the other? Only time will tell.

WHAT'S NEXT FOR PLAYBOY

In 2008, Playboy Enterprises sold its DVD sales division and began outsourcing its studio and catalog and e-commerce businesses. In 2009, the company shut down its New York City office and its online gaming operations, and began outsourcing its newsstand sales for *Playboy* magazine and its Special Editions. Ad sales for *Playboy* magazine dropped and online traffic remained relatively flat. At the same time, the television market became more competitive and growth slowed in that business. All was not grim for Playboy Enterprises though. New merchandise was launched, and although sales were down overall, the future looked promising. The Playboy brand was expanding overseas through new licensing opportunities and magazine launches, new mobile ventures and the Playboy venue in Las Vegas were performing well, and a redesigned Playboy.com Web site was developed and debuted in 2009. The new CEO, Scott Flanders, seemed to understand that the brand still held immense value and the future held opportunities. In the June 2009 press release announcing his appointment as CEO of Playboy Enterprises, Flanders said, "This is an exciting time to assume the role of CEO. The evolution of the media industry and the global recession's effect on consumer spending intensify the need for

A BRAND RISES BACK TO THE TOP—THE 2000s AND THE FUTURE

a creative and effective business model." All hope was not lost, and Playboy Enterprises set forth with three primary goals for the future:

1. Grow its licensing business, particularly with items targeted to women.
2. Create content for integrated media platforms (television, Internet, mobile, print), particularly targeted to younger audiences.
3. Develop international opportunities, particularly for publishing and merchandising and in international markets such as Latin America, India, and China.

Playboy Enterprises also planned to expand its efforts in the mobile marketplace in the future, and Playboy venues similar to the one at the Palms Casino Resort in Las Vegas were already in the development stages for London, England, and Macau, China. Perhaps more surprising, the company planned to continue its reliance on subscription-based income.

BOX 19.1 Skoal and Playboy

For its January 2009 55th anniversary edition, *Playboy* magazine entered into an advertising campaign with Skoal smokeless tobacco unlike anything Playboy had done before. In "Skoal Builds Playboy," the last 12 pages of the January 2009 issue of *Playboy* were dedicated completely to thanking the Skoal brotherhood (or "customers"). Even the back-page, a coveted advertising position, belonged to Skoal, and the *Playboy* cover model, Kara Monaco, was photographed lying on a bed and covered in Skoal tins in a hat tip to the famous *American Beauty* movie poster in which Mena Suvari is covered in rose petals.

Those 12 pages were the result of a user-generated content campaign that Playboy and Skoal developed. Between July and August 2008, Skoal customers were invited to select the content for the 12-page spread on Skoalbrotherhood.com by voting for a celebrity interview subject, selecting a question for a Playmate, submitting jokes, and voting for a Skoal model to be featured in a pictorial. In addition, the 1,000 most active participants on the Web site as part of the "Skoal Builds Playboy" campaign were listed as editors in *Playboy* magazine, and anyone who participated in the promotion and requested a copy of the magazine received one for free. Once the magazine hit newsstands, visitors to the Skoalbrotherhood.

> com Web site could enter to win a trip to a popular Playboy event, Playboy's VIP Players Pajama and Lingerie Party in Los Angeles.
>
> The social media campaign was a big success and boosted traffic to the Skoalbrotherhood.com site by 382% in comparison to the first 6 months of 2008. The goal for Playboy was to turn more Skoal customers into Playboy readers by introducing them to the magazine in a unique way (at the time of the campaign, only 16% of Playboy readers used smokeless tobacco products, so the Skoal audience presented significant opportunities for Playboy). The "Skoal Builds Playboy" campaign was supported with ads in other men's magazines, point-of-purchase displays, on-pack advertising, online and direct mail ads and in *Playboy*.

The strategy worked in the past and made the company somewhat resistant to economic factors, however, it is difficult to predict if this could end up being the company's Achilles heel. Attempts were being made in 2009 to increase the amount of advertising space on Playboy.com, and new advertising partnerships were being created for *Playboy* magazine. For example, Skoal purchased a 12-page special section in the 55th anniversary edition of *Playboy* which included an online viral component that was very popular (see Box 19.1 for details about the Skoal campaign), but it appears that subscription revenue will continue to be the predominant income generator for Playboy Enterprises. In a changing world that has easy access to information, this strategy could be very limiting to the company's long-term growth prospects.

Playboy is hindered by its own legacy and a brand position in desperate need of a makeover. Despite Hugh Hefner's consistent messages that Playboy is about a lifestyle, not sex, consumers have always tied sex to the brand first and foremost. It's a connection that worked well for the company for many years when sexually explicit content was hard to come by, but in a modern world where sex is everywhere, the positioning adds very little value. As part of an overall brand repositioning strategy that differentiates Playboy from its competitors and creates a more contemporary brand promise, the company needs to find a new way to add value to consumers' lives above and beyond what they can find anywhere else. Success will depend on whether or not Playboy Enterprises invests the time and resources into educating consumers about the brand's modernized positioning and value proposition, building relationships with target customer segments, and resisting the urge to rely on the brand's inherent equity in order to achieve long-term growth and more importantly, to survive another decade.

The question is this—will Playboy Enterprises view its decline in the first decade of the 21st century as an opportunity, and will the company make the changes necessary to meet the needs of consumers in a world that changes faster than the company has been able to keep up in the past? Certainly, the company has the brand power to survive. Consumers are still very much interested in the Playboy brand; however, it stands more as a category placeholder today than a category leader or driver. Playboy Enterprises needs to take the necessary steps to develop products and services that achieve two goals—differentiate the brand from competitors and fulfill consumers' wants and needs from the brand. Remember the fundamental business truth—it's far easier to create a product to meet an existing need than it is to create a perceived need to meet the business objectives of an existing product. While it seems evident that Playboy will never be as big as it was in the late 1960s and early 1970s again, simply because the world has changed and its core product, sex, has become a commodity, that doesn't mean there isn't a place for Playboy in the marketplace. Consumers have spoken. It's up to Playboy Enterprises now.

Bibliography

"1950s," http://en.wikipedia.org/wiki/1950s.
"1960s," http://en.wikipedia.org/wiki/1960s.
"1970s," http://en.wikipedia.org/wiki/1970s.
"1980s," http://en.wikipedia.org/wiki/1980s.
"1990s," http://en.wikipedia.org/wiki/1990s.
"2000–2009," http://en.wikipedia.org/wiki/2000–2009.
Abramovich, G. (16 Jan. 2009) "Playboy Exec: Original Content is King," http://www.mobilemarketer.com/cms/news/content/2465.html.
Ackerman, R. (10 Dec. 2008) "Woman on the Verge," http://www.forbes.com/markets/2008/12/10/playboy-hefner-entertainment-markets-face-cx_ra_1208autofacescan02.html.
Ali, R. (15 Oct. 2008) "Playboy Enterprises Does Restructuring; Shutting DVD Division for Online Focus; 80 Positions Will Go," http://www.forbes.com/2008/10/15/playboy-enterprises-restructures-tech-cx_pco_1015paidcontent.html.
Altman, A. (2 Dec. 2008) "Girlie Mags," http://www.time.com/time/arts/article/0,8599,1862878,00.html.
"Attorney General's Commission on Pornography—Final Report." (Jul. 1986). http://www.porn-report.com/.
Bercovici, J. (19 Dec. 2008) "What Comes Next for Playboy Enterprises?" http://www.portfolio.com/views/blogs/mixed-media/2008/12/19/what-comes-next-for-playboy-enterprises.
Bhushan, A. (8 Dec. 2008) "Christie Hefner to Step Down as Playboy Enterprises, Inc. Chairman and CEO: Jerome Kern Appointed Interim Chairman," http://ceoworld.biz/ceo/2008/12/08/christie-hefner-to-step-down-as-playboy-enterprises-inc-chairman-and-ceo-jerome-kern-appointed-interim-chairman/.

BIBLIOGRAPHY

Binn, J. (May/June 2009) "Hugh's That Guy," http://www.la-confidential-magazine.com/LAC_MJ09_057_HUG.html.

Boucher, G. (4 Jan. 2009) "Playboy Founder Hugh Hefner's First True Love was Movies," http://www.latimes.com/entertainment/news/la-ca-hefner4-2009jan04,0,7679368.story.

"A Brand with an Iconic Quality." (1 Jan. 2008). http://www.leadersmag.com/issues/2008.1_jan/hefner.html.

"Bunny Redux." (4 Aug. 1975). http://www.time.com/time/magazine/article/0,9171,913396,00.html.

Burns, G. (8 Dec. 2008) "Christie Hefner Talks to the Tribune about Leaving Playboy," http://www.chicagotribune.com/business/chi-hefner-interview-dec8,0,123319.story.

Burns, G. (30 Jan. 2009) "Fresh Face, Old Hand Join Playboy as Christie Hefner Exits," http://www.chicagotribune.com/business/columnists/chi-fri-burns-playboy-jan30,0,6911610.column.

Califia, P. (1986) "The Obscene, Disgusting, and Vile Meese Commission Report," http://eserver.org/cultronix/califia/meese/.

Carpenter, T. (5 Nov. 1980) "Death of a Playmate," *The Village Voice.* Nov 5–11, 1980 Vol XXV. N0. 45.

Clifford, S. (9 Dec. 2008) "Departure but Little Change at Playboy?" http://www.iht.com/articles/2008/12/09/technology/playboy.php.

Collins, S. (4 Dec. 2003) "Dialogue with Hugh and Christie Hefner," http://www.hollywoodreporter.com/hr/search/article_display.jsp?vnu_content_id=2044729.

Corr, A. (12 Jan. 2009) "Skoal Can Hides Playmate Cans," http://www.mediapost.com/publications/?fa=Articles.showArticleHomePage&art_aid=98179.

Crown Media Holdings, Inc. Web site—Investor Relations FAQs. http://phx.corporate-ir.net/phoenix.zhtml?c=103320&p-irol-faq.

Dobrow, L. (29 Jan. 2009) "Magazines Worth Saving, or Mourning," http://adage.com/mediaworks/article?article_id=134186.

Edwards, D.M. (1992) "Politics and Pornography: A Comparison of the Findings of the President's Commission and the Meese Commission and the Resulting Response," http://home.earthlink.net/~durangodave/html/writing/Censorship.htm.

"FHM." http://en.wikipedia.org/wiki/Fhm.

Friedman, J. (19 Mar. 2008) "Playboy's Hefner: The Luckiest Guy on the Planet," http://www.marketwatch.com/News/Story/playboys-hugh-hefner-life-sweeter/story.aspx?guid=%7bCBCC3444-0B95-4678-8FF6-9F3D0DB1742B%7d&print=true&dist=printMidSection.

Friedman, J. (26 Mar. 2008) "The Playboy Mansion: A Disneyland for Adults," http://www.marketwatch.com/news/story/playboy-mansion-disneyland-adults/story.aspx?guid=%7b739E7788-B821-4613-97D9-57AC9675BB4F%7d&print=true&dist=printMidSection.

BIBLIOGRAPHY

Friedman, J. (8 Dec. 2008) "Playboy Shares Soar as Christie Hefner Resigns," http://www.marketwatch.com/news/story/story.aspx?guid=%7BBC049DD7%2D8D49%2D4EAA%2DB4D5%2DEB87072B8A43%7D&siteid=rss&print=true&dist=printMidSection.

Gardner, G. and Bellows, J. (2007) 80. Naperville, IL: Sourcebooks, Inc.

Goodman, D. (18 Dec. 2008) "Hugh Hefner's Teenage Sons Say Playboy Needs New Direction," http://www.reuters.com/article/lifestyleMolt/idUSTRE4BH0S720081218.

Groucutt, J. (2005) Foundations of Marketing. London: Palgrave Macmillan.

Hallmark Channel Web site, http://www.hallmarkchannel.com.

Hansel, M. (11 Nov. 2008) "Smart Marketers Should be All Ears to Playboy Strategy," http://www.inbusinesslasvegas.com/2008/11/21/retailreal.html.

"Hef's Bio Woes." (2 Dec. 1974). http://www.people.com/people/archive/article/0,,20064716,00.html.

Hein, K. (15 Dec. 2008) "Skoal Brotherhood Shapes 'Playboy' Anniversary Edition," http://www.brandweek.com/bw/content_display/news-and-features/promotion/e3iaa83ea53feec6959ef46f578a2d48c42.

"Hooters Continues to Eye Airline." (3 Sep. 2002). http://money.cnn.com/2002/09/03/news/companies/hooters/.

Hooters MasterCard Web site, http://www.hooterscard.com.

Hooters Web site, http://www.hooters.com.

"Hugh M. Hefner." http://www.imdb.com/name/nm00050005/.

"Hustler." http://en.wikipedia.org/wiki/Hustler.

Hylton, W.S. (1 Jun. 2002) "What I've Learned: Hugh Hefner," http://www.esquire.com/features/what-ive-learned/ESQ0602-JUN_WIL.

"Is the Party Over for Playboy?" (14 Oct. 2008), http://www.independent.co.uk/news/people/profiles/is-the-party-over-for-playboy-960143.html.

Jackson, G. (19 May 1983). "ABC News Classics: Hugh Hefner," ABC News Productions, Inc.

Kaplan, D. (9 Dec. 2008) "Playboy's Hunt for New CEO; 'We Don't Know How Long It Will Take,'" http://www.washingtonpost.com/wp-dyn/content/article/2008/12/09/AR2008120902154.html.

Landrum, G.N. (2004) Entrepreneurial Genius: The Power of Passion. Naples, FL: Brendan Kelly Publishing Inc.

Luscombe, B. (24 Jan. 2009) "Playboy Shows Signs of Withdrawal," http://www.time.com/time/nation/article/0,8599,1873780,00.html.

Macavinta, C. (30 Jul. 1998) "Playboy Online Revenues Double," http://news.cnet.com/Playboy-Online-revenues-double/2100-1001_3-213929.html.

MacMillan, R. (6 Nov. 2008) "Playboy's Ad Sales Drop, Shares Tumble," http://www.reuters.com/article/idUSTRE4A55JE20081106.

Mauro, T. (23 May 2000) "Supreme Court Brings 'Clarity' to Laws Governing Cable TV," http://www.freedomforum.org/templates/document.asp?documentID=12529.

BIBLIOGRAPHY

"Maxim." http://en.wikipedia.org/wiki/Maxim_(magazine).

McKay, H. (28 Apr. 2009) "Exclusive: Hugh Hefner Wants the 'Love of His Life' Holly Madison to Return to Mansion," http://www.foxnews.com/story/0,2933,518219,00.html.

"Meese Report." http://en.wikipedia.org/wiki/Meese_Report.

Munk, N. (12 Jul. 1999) "Wall Street Follies," http://ninamunk.com/documents/wallstreetfollies.htm.

Nakashima, R. (2006) "The Bunny is Back," http://www.palms.com/items/press/AP%20Playboy%20Club.pdf.

"The Naked Truth." (1999). http://www.contextmag.com/setFrameRedirect.asp?src=/archives/199812/Feature0TheNakedTruth.asp.

Negus-Viveiros, B. (1 Jan. 2009) "Mary Kay's Rhonda Shasteen Works on a Brand Makeover," http://directmag.com/casehistories/0109-shasteen-works-makeover/.

"Oral History Transcript: Christie Hefner." (Oct. 2002). http://www.cablecenter.org/education/library/oralHistoryDetails.cfm?id=106.

Palmeri, C. (8 Dec. 2008) "Christie Hefner is Leaving Playboy," http://www.businessweek.com/bwdaily/dnflash/content/dec2008/db2008128_900186.htm?campaign_id=rss_daily.

Petersen, J.R. (1999) The Century of Sex: Playboy's History of the Sexual Revolution; 1900–1999. New York, NY: Grove Press.

Phillips, R. (1992) "Expanding Your Consumer Franchise," http://findarticles.com/p/articles/mi_m3065/is_nGUIDE_v21/ai_12254285/print?tag=artBody;col1.

Piccolo, S. (2003) "Gaming in Atlantic City . . . A History of Legalized Gambling in New Jersey," http://www.ccgtcc.com/piccolosachistory.pdf.

Playboy 2000: The Party Continues. (2001). DVD. Beverly Hills, CA: Playboy Entertainment Group, Inc.

"Playboy Bunnies Hop Back to UK." (13 Jan. 2008). http://business.timesonline.co.uk/tol/business/industry_sectors/leisure/article4322711.ece.

Playboy Enterprises Web site
  "Biography Hugh M. Hefner," (Jun. 2008).
  "Hugh Hefner Awards and Honors," (1969–2002).
  "Hugh M. Hefner First Amendment Awards." (Dec. 2008).
  "Playboy Enterprises Appoints Jimmy Jellinek to New Position of Editorial Director of Playboy Magazine and Playboy.com." (22 Jan. 2009). http://phx.corporate-ir.net/phoenix.zhtml?c=100055&p=irol-newsArticle&ID=1247415&highlight=.
  "Playboy Enterprises Inc. Q3 2008 Earnings Call Transcript. (25 Nov. 2008).
  "Playboy Enterprises, Inc. Anticipates Charges in Fourth Quarter 2008 Results." (22 Jan. 2008). http://phx.corporate-ir.net/phoenix.zhtml?c=100055&p=irol-newsArticle&ID=1247404&highlight=.

BIBLIOGRAPHY

"Playboy Enterprises, Inc. Corporate Overview." (Jun. 2008).
Christie Hefner Biography (Jan. 2009).
Hugh Hefner Timeline (1926–2008).
Playboy Enterprises Annual Report (1999).
Playboy Enterprises Annual Report (2000).
Playboy Enterprises Annual Report (2001).
Playboy Enterprises Annual Report (2002).
Playboy Enterprises Annual Report (2003).
Playboy Enterprises Annual Report (2004).
Playboy Enterprises Annual Report (2005).
Playboy Enterprises Annual Report (2006).
Playboy Enterprises Form 10-K (29 Mar. 1999).
Playboy Enterprises Form 10-K (30 Mar. 2000).
Playboy Enterprises Form 10-K. (14 Mar. 2008).
Playboy FAQ (Dec. 2008).
"Scott Flanders Elected CEO of Playboy Enterprises; David Chemerow Appointed Non-executive Chairman." (1 Jun. 2008). http://playboyenterprises.com/home/content.cfm?content=t_press&packet=9DBE1065-C1C2-4A8A-C4A807C88A5984B2&MmenuFlag=news.
UBS Global Media and Communications Conference Presentation (9 Dec. 2008).
Playboy Gaming Web site, http://www.playboygaming.com/.
"Playboy Goes Public." (27 Sep. 1971). http://www.time.com/time/magazine/article/0,9171,910069,00.html?promoid=googlep.
"Playboy Launches Social Networking Site." (24 Aug. 2007). http://www.foxnews.com/story/0,2933,294254,00.html.
"Playboy Poker to Shut." (23 Jan. 2009). http://www.igamingbusiness.com/article-detail.php?articleID=19810.
"Playboy Posts Loss after Shedding TV Assets." (6 Nov. 2008). http://www.dailyherald.com/story/print/?id=248741.
Poupada, R. (11 Dec. 2008) "28 Questions with Hugh Hefner," http://www.askmen.com/celebs/interview_300/303_hugh_hefner_interview.html.
Powell, A.C. (30 Dec. 1998) "U.S. Appeals Court Rules 1999 CDA Cable TV 'Blocking' Provision Unconstitutional," http://www.firstamendmentcenter.org/news.aspx?id=9282&SearchString="""""Playboy_Entertainment_group""""".
Randall, S. (ed) (2007) The Playboy Interviews: Movers and Shakers. Milwaukie, OR: M Press.
Ries, A. and Ries, L. (2002) The 22 Immutable Laws of Branding. New York, NY: HarperCollins Publishers.
Ries, A. and Trout, J. (1993) The 22 Immutable Laws of Marketing: Violate Them at Your Own Risk. New York, NY: HarperCollins Publishers.

BIBLIOGRAPHY

Rogers, J. (14 Jan. 2009) "Apple's Jobs to Take Medical Leave," http://www.thestreet.com/story/10457956/1/apples-jobs-to-take-medical-leave.html.

Rose, C. (10 Dec. 2003). "Charlie Rose with Joseph Biden; Hugh Hefner and Christie Hefner." DVD. Charlie Rose, Inc.

Santi, A. (23 Oct. 2007) "The Drapers Interview: Christie Hefner," http://www.drapersonline.com/lingerie/driv/2007/10/the_drapers_interview_christie_hefner.html.

Sauer, A.D. (19 May 2003) "Playboy Exposed," http://www.brandchannel.com/features_profile.asp?pr_id=125.

Schwartz, D.G. (Dec. 2006) "Bunny on the Boardwalk," http://www.casinoconnectionac.com/articles/Bunny_on_the_Boardwalk.

Seib, C. (9 Dec. 2008) "Hefner's Daughter Christie Walks Away from Playboy Enterprises," http://business.timesonline.co.uk/tol/business/industry_sectors/media/article5310203.ece.

Sherwood, J. (11 May 2009) "Playboy to Take on World of Warcraft with Bunny-themed MMORG," http://www.reghardware.co.uk/2009/05/11/playboy_manager/.

Skinner, J. (7 Apr. 2006) "Hugh Hefner Reflects on Turning 80," http://www.foxnews.com/story/0,2933,190979,00.html.

Smith, S. (11 Dec. 2008) "Playboy: The Mini-Micro Series," http://www.mediapost.com/publications/?fa=Articles.showArticleHomePage&art_aid=96551.

"Steve Jobs Takes Medical Leave." (15 Jan. 2009). http://tech.yahoo.com/news/nm/20090115/wr_nm/us_apple_tech_1.

Swartz, J. and Acohido, B. (14 Jan. 2009) "Apple CEO Steve Jobs Takes Medical Leave until June," http://www.usatoday.com/tech/news/2009-01-14-steve-jobs_N.htm?csp=34.

"THQ Developing Mobile Playboy Games." (28 Jan. 2008). http://blastmagazine.com/the-magazine/technology/2008/01/thq-developing-mobile-playboy-games/.

"Tobacco Companies Paid Movie Stars Millions in Celebrity Endorsement Deals." (24 Sep. 2008). British Media Journal. http://www.sciencecodex.com/tobacco_companies_paid_movie_stars_millions_in_celebrity_endorsement_deals.

Tommy Constantine Racing Web site, http://www.tommyconstantine.com/.

Tybout, A.M. and Calkins, T. (eds) (2005) Kellogg on Branding. Hoboken, NJ: John Wiley & Sons.

"United States et al. v. Playboy Entertainment Group, Inc." (decided 22 May 2000). http://caselaw.lp.findlaw.com/scripts/getcase.pl?navby=case&court=us&vol=529&page=803.

Watts, S. (2008) Mr. Playboy: Hugh Hefner and the American Dream. DVD. Hoboken, NJ: John Wiley & Sons.

Index

advertisers
   bundling packages for, 146
   consistency of branding and, 26, 27–8, 79–80, 144–5
   early interest in Playboy, 23
   revenue from, 131
   "Skoal Builds Playboy" campaign, 174–5
African American Playmate, 51
AIDS, 97
American Express celebrity endorsements, 130
Anderson, Pamela, 19, 128–9
Apple brand, 18–19, 78, 161–2
Atlantic City casino, 104–5, 113–14
AT&T brand, 44

Baby Boomer Generation, 48
bait-and-hook, 16
banning of *Playboy* magazine, 23
Big Bunny jet, 59, 87
Billboard's top 40 list, 138
Blackberry brand, 61
Bogdanovich, Peter, 112–13
Boston Market brand, 77
brand advocates, 160
brand buzz, 25, 73
brand champions, 161–2
   Hefner as, 24–5, 86, 87–9, 120, 160, 172–3

brand development
   consistency of, 26, 27–8, 79–80, 144–5
   endorsements and, 128–30
   expansion without restraints, 83–4
   extensions, 28, 40, 41–3
   persistency in, 26, 28
   power brands, 34
   relationship branding, 17–19, 146–7, 164
   steps of, 23–8
   see also Playboy brand
brand focus, 41, 43–5
brand guardians, 160
Buick celebrity endorsements, 130
bundled advertising, 146
bunnies, 38, 51, 52, 84
bunny logo, 11
Burger King brand, 76

Carpenter, Teresa, 112–13
category extensions, 99
celebrity endorsements, 116–17, 128–30
challenging brands, 100–1
Cisneros Group, 134, 136
Clinton-Lewinsky scandal, 126
Clorox brand repositioning, 110
Club Jenna, 152
cluster analysis, 91–2

INDEX

Coca-Cola brand, 81, 98
college students, 147
communication and branding, 26–7
competitive market positioning strategies, 76–7, 78–9
Conrad, Kimberley, 120, 141
conservative politics, 21
consistency of branding, 26, 27–8, 79–80, 144–5
consumers
  cluster analysis, 91–2
  emotional involvement, 32, 60–3, 164
  giving control to, 49, 171
  loyalty of, 79–80, 164
  relationship branding and, 17–19, 146–7, 164
contraction of brand, 43–5
core value proposition, 58
corporate giving, *see* Playboy Foundation
costs of new products, 41–2
cult brands, 53, 60–3
curiosity and brand buzz, 25

Daily Illini, 8
Daniels, Derick, 107
defensive positioning strategies, 78–9
definition step of branding, 26–7
Disney brand, 30–1, 99
Dove brand, 99

economies of scale, 145–6
emotions of consumers, 32, 60–3, 164
escapism, 68–9
ESPN strategies, 145
Esquire magazine, 6, 9
experience brands, 29–31, 31–3, 37–40, 164–5
experiential marketing, 164–5

FBI investigations, 23
feminist battles, 51, 52
Feminist Movement, 69–70
FHM, 131, 143

Flanders, Scott, 172, 173–4
free speech, 50, 137

The Gap brand, 100
Generation Jones, 68
Generation X, 127–8
Generation Y, 153, 157–8
The Girls Next Door, 156–7
globalization, 99
Google brand, 78–9, 145
"The Great Repression," 97–8

Hallmark Channel, 119
Hanes celebrity endorsements, 130
Hard Rock Cafe brand, 40
Hardee's, 77
Harley Davidson brand, 99
Heffer, Goo, 6, 8
Hefner, Christie
  birth, 9
  early years with Playboy, 90–1, 106–7
  executive roles, 107–9, 110–11
  refocusing on Playboy brand, 115–18
  Section 505 views, 137
  stepping down, 160, 163
  strategic planning in 1990s, 133
Hefner, Cooper, 160, 163, 172
Hefner, Glenn, 4
Hefner, Grace, 4
Hefner, Hugh
  absence from operational management, 71, 74, 109–10, 133
  appearances in movies/television, 55, 124, 152–3, 157
  arrest on obscenity charges, 50
  awards/honors, 89, 114, 142, 163
  as brand champion, 24–5, 86, 87–9, 120, 160, 172–3
  business skills *vs.* instinct, 15, 113–14
  as celebrity, 55, 58–9
  children of, 123–4, 160, 163, 172, *see also* Hefner, Christie
  control over *Playboy*, 16–17, 22, 39–40
  early life, 3–9

INDEX

Hefner, Hugh – *continued*
  feminists and, 51, 52, 69–70
  Hitler comparison, 105
  marijuana support by, 96
  personality traits, 3, 5, 39
  political views, 37, 45, 53, 96
  protests against, 49–50, 96
  regrets, 173
  reinventions: as celebrity, 58–9;
    as family man, 120, 123–4; for
    healthy lifestyle, 115; as playboy,
    24, 142; in teenage years, 5–6
  Stratton murder and, 112–13
  wives: Kimberley Conrad, 120, 141;
    Millie Williams, 9, 10, 24
Hefner, Marston, 160, 163, 172
Hooters brand, 83–4
Hugh M. Hefner Awards, 91
Hustler, 77, 78, 108–9
Hyundai brand repositioning, 110

IBM loss of focus, 44
inclusive brand strategy, 60, 171
integrated marketing strategies,
  144–7, 166
integrated media platforms, 174
Interns, 158, 169
iPhones brand, 61, 99

Jack Daniels brand, 40
jet (Big Bunny), 59, 87
Jobs, Steve, 161–2

The Killing of the Unicorn, 113
Kinsey, Alfred, 8

laddie magazines, 131, 143
licensing business, 115–18, 134–5, 174
line extensions, 98
long-term strategic planning, 100,
  132, 140, 144
Lownes, Victor, 82, 84–5
loyalty of customers, 79–80

Macbeth, 83
macro environment

conservatism of 1980s, 95–8
  impact on merchandising, 154–5
  leveraging examples, 53
  Playboy's failure to address, 100
  political climate of 1960s, 45–6
  post-war years of 1950s, 13, 21–2
  societal unrest of 1970s, 68–70, 89
market leaders, 76, 100–1
marketing, experiential, 164–5
marketplace positioning strategies,
  76–7, 78–9
Martha Stewart brand, 101
Mary Kay brand, 162
Maxim, 131, 143
McCarthy, Jenny, 129
McDonald's restaurants, 76
Meese Commission, 105–6
merchandising business, 115–18,
  138–9, 154–5
micro environment of 1950s, 22
Microsoft, 78
mobile programs, 157–8, 169
Monroe, Marilyn, 10–11, 16, 128
movies, 83
Mozilla's Firefox, 78
multimedia events, 145–6
Mustang brand cult, 61

National Geographic brand, 116
Nazi literature compared to *Playboy*, 70
New Beetle brand, 101
New Coke brand, 81
new markets, 99
new products, costs of, 41–2
new uses for products, 99
niche audiences, 45

Obama, Barack, 60
offensive positioning strategies, 78
Oiu magazine, 77
online competition, 143–4, 147, 170–1
overexpansion of brands, 166

Palms Casino Resort, 154
Penthouse, 75–80, 91, 108–9
Pepsi brand, 53

185

INDEX

perfume merchandising, 116–17
personalization by consumers, 60–3
Phillips, Reed, 118
pioneer brands, 76, 100–1
Playboy: The Mansion, 153
Playboy Advisor, 48
Playboy After Dark, 45, 59
Playboy brand
   combating decline in 1980s, 98–102
   consistency and, 16–17, 27, 39–40, 144–6
   drug investigations and, 70–1
   extensions of, 28–34, 72, 103–5, 151–8, 165–6
   focus of, 41, 43, 85, 107–9, 115–18
   future of, 171, 175–6
   global markets, 55–6, 67, 131–2, 134–5, 136, 138–9, 174
   growth in 1950s, 22–5
   Hefner as symbol of, 70–1, 86, 125, 141
   historical overview, 163–6
   Hollywood celebrities and, 19, 56–8, 59, 87–8
   inclusiveness of, 50–1, 171
   loss of focus in 1970s, 72, 79–80
   market saturation, 34
   merchandising, 138–9
   obstacles in early days, 20
   peak of, 74
   as pioneer, 75, 78–9, 100–1
   profit lows, 75
   rebuilding in 2000s, 166–7, 168–9
   restructuring in 1970s, 83–6
   revenue and, 170
   sexual revolution and, 37, 45
   as symbol of dichotomies, 125
Playboy Clubs, 29, 37–8, 83, 107
Playboy Cyber Club, 140
Playboy Enterprises
   casinos and gaming, 55–6, 85, 103–5, 113–14, 154, 155–6, 170
   future of, 173–6
   lawsuit against Meese Commission, 106

online competition, 143–4, 147, 170–1
   problems in 2000s, 168–70
   reactionary positions, 159, 168–9
   revival in 2000s, 151–4
   Section 505 court case, 137
   succession plan, 172
   see also Hefner, Christie; Hefner, Hugh; timelines of Playboy history
Playboy Forum, 50
Playboy Foundation, 56, 57, 91
Playboy Jazz Festival, 31, 90
Playboy magazine
   anniversary celebration (50th), 156
   circulation, 12, 14, 37, 72, 130–2
   competition, 75–82, 91, 108–9, 131, 143–4
   content, 16, 27, 38–9, 56, 80, 125
   early promotional tactics, 15–19
   early success, 12, 14–15
   initial investment, 10–11
   lifestyle image, 12–15, 16–19, 24–5, 109, 125, 171
   naming of, 11
   Nazi comparison, 105
   protests against, 49, 69–70, 96, 105–6
   racial inclusiveness, 50–1
   repositioning back to roots, 81–2, 108–11
   U.S. Postal Service court battle, 23
Playboy Mansions
   as family home, 123, 124
   political events, 90
   purchase of, 29, 88
   re-opening (1998), 142
Playboy Modeling Agency, 31
Playboy on Campus, 147
Playboy online, 139–40, 169–70
Playboy Panel, 49
Playboy Philosophy, 49–50, 126
Playboy Resorts, 59
"Playboy's Political Preference Chart," 53
Playboy television/movies
   expansion in 1990s, 135–8
   Girls Next Door, 156–7

INDEX

Playboy television/movies – *continued*
  multimedia events, 145–6
  online content competing with, 155
  pay-per-view, 118–20
  Playboy After Dark, 45, 59
  Playboy Channel, 108, 135–6
  Playboy's Penthouse, 29
  Playboy TV, 134, 152
  Spice Entertainment, 136
Playboy Tours, 31
Playboy U, 157
Playboy venue, 154
Playmates, 17, 51, 90–1
Polaroid brand, 99–100
politics, 43, 45–6, 47–8, 49
popular culture, 63
pornography
  Hustler, 77, 78, 108–9
  Internet content as, 143–4
  Meese Report on, 105–6
  Oiu magazine, 77
  Penthouse, 75–80, 91, 108–9
power brands, 34
primary level of brand experience, 33
profitability and brand champions, 161–2
Pubic Wars, 79
publicity and controversy, 25, 49–50, 88
Publisher's Department Corporation, 9
Puritanism, 3–4

quality content, 16
Quaternary level of brand experience, 32, 33

reality television, 156–7
relationship branding, 17–19, 146–7, 164
risks of new products, 42

Saturn brand, 30, 81
Secondary level of brand experience, 33
Section 505 of the Telecommunications Act (1996), 136, 137, 152

segmentation of customers, 91–2
sex
  freedom/tolerance in society, 125–6
  proliferation of content, 131, 143–4
  "Sex in America" study, 124
  sexual revolution, 37, 45
  see also pornography
Sexual Behavior in the Human Male, 8
Shaft, 8
Silent Generation, 13, 14
"Skoal Builds Playboy" campaign, 174–5
Smith, Anna Nicole, 129
Spanish-language Playboy network, 136
Spice Entertainment, 136, 140, 151–2
Springmaid advertising, 23
Starbucks brand, 32
Steinem, Gloria, 51, 52, 70
Stratten, Dorothy, 112–13
subscription video-on-demand (SVOD), 152

tease marketing, 16
technology
  competition based on, 143–4, 147, 159, 170–1
  Generation X and, 127–8
  influences, 21–2
  Web site of Playboy, 139–40, 169–70
Telecommunications Act of 1996, 136, 137, 152
Tertiary level of brand experience, 32–3
That Toddlin' Town, 9
three Ss of customer loyalty, 79–80
timelines of Playboy history
  1950s, 1
  1960s, 35–6
  1970s, 65, 66
  1980s, 93
  1990s, 121
  2000s, 149–50
tobacco celebrity endorsements, 130
Toyota Prius brand, 53

INDEX

U.S. Postal Service court battle, 23

video games, 153
video-on-demand (VOD), 152
videos, 138
Volkswagen Beetle brand, 101

Web site of Playboy, 139–40, 169–70
Wendy's, 76
Williams, Mildred, 7, 9
women and Playboy brand, 139